Miriam

Becoming a Girl of Courage

DANNAH GRESH

with Kindra Stanton & Magnolia Garrett

MOODY PUBLISHERS

CHICAGO

Unless otherwise indicated, all Scripture quotations are taken from the Holy Bible, New Living Translation, copyright © 1996, 2004, 2015 by Tyndale House Foundation. Used by permission of Tyndale House Publishers, Inc., Carol Stream, Illinois 60188. All rights reserved.

Scripture quotations marked ESV are from the ESV® Bible (The Holy Bible, English Standard Version®), copyright © 2001 by Crossway, a publishing ministry of Good News Publishers. Used by permission. All rights reserved.

Edited by Ashleigh Slater
Interior and cover design: Julia Ryan
Cover and interior illustrations: Julia Ryan
Icon jewel page 21: © Shutterstock/babysofja

Library of Congress Cataloging-in-Publication Data

Names: Gresh, Dannah, 1967- author.
Title: Miriam : becoming a girl of courage / Dannah Gresh.
Description: Chicago : Moody Publishers, [2022] I Series: True girl Bible
  studies I Includes bibliographical references. I Audience: Ages 8-12 I
  Summary: "Miriam's life reminds us that a True Girl practices courageous
  leadership right now because a leader is what she's becoming. Though
  leaders are imperfect, God offers us second chances to get things right.
  True Girl Bible Studies help moms and daughters discover how to be women
  after God's own heart"-- Provided by publisher.
Identifiers: LCCN 2021044633 (print) I LCCN 2021044634 (ebook) I ISBN
  9780802422415 (paperback) I ISBN 9780802499370 (ebook)
Subjects: LCSH: Miriam (Biblical figure)--Juvenile literature. I Miriam
  (Biblical figure)--Textbooks. I Christian girls--Religious
  life--Juvenile literature. I BISAC: JUVENILE NONFICTION / Religious /
  Christian / Inspirational I JUVENILE FICTION / Girls & Women
Classification: LCC BS580.M54 G74 2022 (print) I LCC BS580.M54 (ebook) I
  DDC 222/.12--dc23
LC record available at https://lccn.loc.gov/2021044633
LC ebook record available at https://lccn.loc.gov/2021044634

Printed by: Sheridan Book in Chelsea, MI, October 2021

Originally delivered by fleets of horse-drawn wagons, the affordable paperbacks from D. L. Moody's publishing house resourced the church and served everyday people. Now, after more than 125 years of publishing and ministry, Moody Publishers' mission remains the same—even if our delivery systems have changed a bit. For more information on other books (and resources) created from a biblical perspective, go to www.moodypublishers.com or write to:

Moody Publishers
820 N. LaSalle Boulevard
Chicago, IL 60610

1 3 5 7 9 10 8 6 4 2

Printed in the United States of America

Table of Contents

My Notes on Miriam

As you study the life of Miriam, you'll come back to this page to write down important thoughts and observations about her and the most important people in her life. Turn here anytime you learn something you don't want to forget or at the end of each chapter when I remind you.

| _____ | _____ | _____ |
| & _____ | | & _____ |

{ Her Brothers }   { A Prophetess }   { Her Parents }

As we study the life of Miriam, you'll learn five important lessons about courage. Sometimes I will invite you to come back to this page and write down what you're learning.

Courage

········► Fill in the blank!

Courage is _____ _____ _____

_____ even when it's _____

or you are _____.

Courage Lessons

Courage Lesson #1

Courage Lesson #2

Courage Lesson #3

Courage Lesson #4

Courage Lesson #5

INTRODUCTION

How to Study the Bible
(Zooming, Zeroing & Zipping Basics!)

If you've never done a True Girl Bible study,
this introduction is really important.
It will explain our style of studying the Bible.

If you have done a True Girl Bible study before,
you can skip this and go straight to chapter 1.[1]

I'm so glad you've decided to dig into this Bible study on the life of Miriam! If you're here, you may have heard of something called the Bible. After all, it is the bestselling book in all of history! You might even read it every single day! But have you ever stopped and wondered: *What's so special about this book? Wait, what even is the Bible?* Well, my friend, those are very good questions, and I'm so glad you asked.

What is the Bible, Really?

The Bible is the story of God's relationship with His creation. Although it's all bound up together into one book that you can hold, the Bible is actually a collection of a bunch of different books by many ancient writers. These books contain stories, poems, songs, prayers, and more that these people wrote about their experiences with God, or when they saw God's story playing out in front of them. And every word of the Bible is *inspired by God*, which means that God was leading the authors and telling them exactly what to write! That means the Bible is God's Word, so it's the ultimate source of truth! (After all, who knows better than God!)

All Scripture is inspired by God and is useful to teach us what is true and to make us realize what is wrong in our lives. It corrects us when we are wrong and teaches us to do what is right. (2 Timothy 3:16)

Fast-forward to today, and guess what? The authors who wrote down the Bible may not be around anymore, but the Bible certainly is. God's story isn't over yet and is continuing with you! It's true. So, as we participate in the story of God's relationship with His creation, we look to the Bible to find the truth of who God is and who we are meant to be. We can use the Bible to learn what is right and wrong. It teaches us how to walk through life, and how to survive in hard times. It can help us know how to express gladness in good times. And best of all, it teaches us how to have a relationship with the God who loves us so much!

 Your word is a lamp to guide my feet and a light for my path. (Psalm 119:105)

Why do the stories in the Bible matter to you?

As you read through the stories in the Bible, you might think, *"What does this have to do with me?"* The people in the Bible lived a long time ago, across the world from where you may live, and they had totally different experiences. At first look, it may seem like you have nothing in common with the people and places you read about. But don't give up so quickly! Keep looking. These are stories about real people in history who experienced God! The same God that loves you and me now. And that is precisely why *we* study the Bible. So *we* can know how to experience God.

Since the Bible is the Word of God, it is full of truth. But sometimes the truth is tucked away and not easy to see! That's why we roll up our sleeves to study the words carefully. When we do that, we discover the most beautiful parts of it!

Have you ever found a buried treasure?

Imagine this: You've gone on a hike through some woods near your neighborhood. You're stepping on leaves, and you hear *crunch, crunch, crunch*!

But suddenly, you step and hear something more like a *crunch-thud*! You kick the leaves away and look below to find that your trail has been interrupted by something smooth and solid. You're standing on what looks to be the lid of a great big wooden chest. You begin to dig it out and then lift it up. It looks old. You pry it open to discover what's inside, and in it, you find a letter! The letter is dated 50 years ago. It was written by a girl who lived in the same neighborhood you live in, and it's all about what life was like in the neighborhood 50 years ago. She writes about who lived in the neighborhood, their plans for an annual cookout, and then the best part—she writes about a hidden hiking trail to find the best views in the forest!

Wow, you just discovered a really cool look into the history of your neighborhood! You decide to find that hiking trail and follow it up to the very top and discover a beautiful view of your neighborhood that you've never seen before.

The Bible is kind of like that letter. Yes, it's very old! (Thousands of years old, in fact!) But it tells us the story of how God loves His people in this world and even helps us see things differently if we follow the trails of those who've lived and walked before us. There is so much we can learn from it and apply to our own lives.

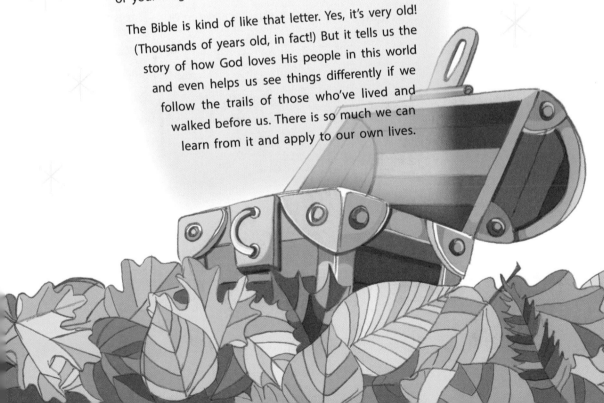

How do we study the Bible?

What do I mean by "study"? There are a couple of things we can do to help us understand the Bible. We can **ZOOM OUT** or **ZOOM IN!**

ZOOM OUT

One way to get a better understanding of what the Bible means is to look at the *context.*

·······▶ { context: **the background of the story.** }

To see the context, we "zoom out" from the story and check out what else was going on in the background. We work to understand the time, place, and people to get a better big picture view of the story—kind of like walking up that secret path to get an above-the-valley view of your neighborhood. We ask questions like this:

- ★ **Who** was there?
- ★ **What** else was happening at that time?
- ★ **Where** did it happen?
- ★ **When** did it happen?
- ★ **Why** did God allow it in their lives?

The answers help us understand the story better! Sometimes the people in the Bible were in circumstances that we don't understand unless we zoom out. This is why it's

so wonderful to read through large sections of the Bible and why I'm so glad you've chosen to study Miriam's story with me. You'll see just how important context is in understanding it.

ZOOM IN

Another way to gain a better understanding of what something in the Bible means to us is to look at the *particulars*.

> ·······➤ { **particulars: the details of the story.** }

To see the details, we dig deep in specific places—like when you step on a treasure chest and lean down to dig it out and lift it up. To see details, we "zoom in" on a word or a phrase to figure out what it really means.

That gets a little tricky when you're studying the Bible. Did you know that it wasn't originally written in English? Most of Miriam's story comes from the Old Testament, which was first written in a language called Hebrew.

> ·······➤ { **Hebrew: the original language the Old Testament was written in.** }

Hebrew has much more descriptive words than the English language does. If I told you I put my baby brother in a basket, you might think that was a perfectly sweet way to give a baby a nap. But if I said that I was placing him in an ark (or boat), you might get something different from what I told you. You might think, *"Oh wow! Why does the baby need to be in an ark!? Is he going to be safe in the water?"*

Just like that, you understand a little more about what I am trying to say. You realize that there's a rescue story unfolding. That's what happens when we zoom in on a word. The original Hebrew word might mean "an ark-basket," and early Christians might have translated that to say "basket." By looking back at the Hebrew language, we sometimes get a more specific explanation of what the author was trying to say and a better picture of what is happening in the story!

When we zoom in to understand the particulars—including specific words—as we study Miriam's life, we'll get a much clearer, close-up shot of what's happening in the story.

{ In this Bible study, we will **zoom out** and **zoom in** to learn from the life of Miriam! }

Welcome to Inductive Bible Study

All of this zooming is really a fun way to enter into what's called the inductive method of Bible study. Some people use big, boring words to learn how to study the Bible, but I think it should be fun. (I just want ya to know you're learning a method with a name.) Here are the three basics steps we'll use to do inductive Bible study:

➤ Zoom In & Out—Who? What? Where? When? Why?

ZOOMING is the most time-consuming part of Bible study. As you observe, you ask and answer a lot of questions. As we examine the life of Miriam, I'll ask the questions, and you get to answer them. (We'll make this fun with quizzes, puzzles, and cool clues.) Sometimes we'll clearly be zooming out. And other times we'll clearly be zooming in. But sometimes it's a big mixture of both at the same time.

ZERO IN: What does it mean?

Once you've considered the *context* (by zooming out) and the *particulars* (by zooming in), you need to think a little harder to figure out *why* this story or truth is in the Bible and what it means for us today. You need to ZERO IN, or focus on what it might mean *for you*. Once again, I'll help you do this with questions. You get to fill in the answers!

ZIP IT UP: What does God want me to do with it?

To complete your study, you'll need to respond to God. After all, the Bible contains His words . . . so when you read it . . . well, that's kind of like one side of a conversation. Now it's time to prepare to obey or agree with or even question God. (Sometimes, a girl needs more information to understand. It's OK to ask God questions.) You'll end your study time by talking to God about what you've learned so you can ask Him what to do with what you've discovered. After all, you've got to ZIP IT UP.

What You'll Need

⭐ Your Bible (you won't actually use it a lot, but that's because I'm keeping this Bible study simple. All of the verses you'll need are printed right in this book. But I want you to get in the habit of having your very own treasured Bible on-hand and marking up your Bible as you study!).

⭐ This copy of *Miriam: Becoming a Girl of Courage*

⭐ Some colored markers or pencils

Got 'em? OK. Let's jump right into Miriam's story. I hope you're as excited as I am!

CHAPTER 1

✳ What Is Courage?

Imagine you're a superhero! It's up to you to save all girls everywhere from Captain Liar Pants. He spends his days shooting globs of sticky feelings at every single human he sees. These no-good, horrible, very bad emotions stick like glue. And the victims of Captain Liar Pants never even know what hits them! Before they realize it, they're trapped in a web of lies like a fly gets stuck in a spider's web.

Thankfully, you possess what just might be the world's best superhero gadget: the Megaphone of Truth! All you have to do is tie on your True Girl cape and blare the truth for all to hear.

Suddenly, the traps Captain Liar Pants has set for all girls everywhere have no power. One by one, the webs fall away, and the girls are rescued. A great shout of victory goes up into the air as Captain Liar Pants slinks off into the darkness.

Superpowers, daring acts, mortal combat, and damsels in distress! These are all things that come to mind when we think about the word *courage*. But let me ask you something: Is this what *real* courage looks like in *real* life?

Let's start zooming!

Zoom In & Out—Who? What? Where? When? Why?

Zoom waaaaaayyyy out with me and you will see that the timeline of Miriam's story begins in the land of Egypt. The Israelites moved there during a famine. For many, many, many years God's people called this place their home. In fact, they'd been there soooo long that they kept having more and more babies. And now, there were a whole lot of them!

Pharaoh, the ruler of Egypt, didn't like that one bit. So, he made them become his slaves. And still, they kept having babies!

So, Pharaoh came up with a horrific idea: "I'll kill all the baby boys."

Talk about villains! This guy was bad.

But, there were good people in this story too, and one of them was a very young girl named Miriam.

Wait, wait, wait!

Let's slow it all down.

Before we start looking for the theme of courage in Miriam's life, we need to be sure we understand what courage *is*. And what it *isn't*.

What is REAl courage?

Dannah & Autumn

My daughter Autumn lived in China and spoke only Mandarin when we met and adopted her at the age of 14. She became a part of our family when she was a teenager! That's kind of unusual, right?

Before we could bring her home, she had to stand ALONE before a judge in a Chinese court of law and declare that she wanted to be adopted. That was scary! Then she had to get onto an airplane with people who could not speak her language and fly far away from everyone and everything she knew and she felt all ALONE. Boy, was that scary! Then she had to get onto an airplane with her new parents who could not speak her language and we arrived in the United States, she had to go ALONE (again) into a private room with a customs police officer and say that she wanted to enter this new country with a new family that she didn't even really know. When we arrived home, everything was new and . . . well, frightening. Even our enormous dog, Stormie, was probably a little bit scary.

The most courageous person I know is my daughter Autumn.

Who's the most courageous person YOU know? Write their name in the award below.

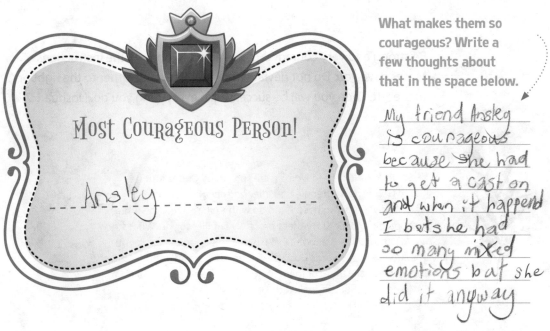

MOST COURAGEOUS PERSON!

Ansley

What makes them so courageous? Write a few thoughts about that in the space below.

My friend Ansley is courageous because she had to get a cast on and when it happend I bet she had so many mixed emotions but she did it anyway

In the Bible, God tells us to have courage. But how can we be courageous if we don't know what it is in the first place?

True courage can be difficult to define and explain. And if we aren't careful, we will begin to believe the lies that the world tells us about it.

So, before I tell you what it *is*, let me tell you what it's *not*. Let's take a look at five lies you may be believing about courage. I'm no superhero, but I'm getting out my megaphone of truth, the Bible! And I hope God uses it to set you free.

LIE #1: Courage Is Doing Something Extraordinary.

It's easy to think that in order to be courageous you have to do something extraordinary. According to the dictionary, *extraordinary* means "going beyond what is usual, regular, or customary."[2] This is just a fancy way of saying something is super special, exciting, or important.

 { Extraordinary: super special, exciting, or important. }

While doing something extraordinary for God can certainly be courageous, living a courageous life is actually much simpler than that. Let me explain.

Read Joshua 1:7. Circle the words "strong," "courageous," and "obey."

Be strong and very courageous. Be careful to obey all the instructions Moses gave you. Do not deviate from them, turning either to the right or to the left. Then you will be successful in everything you do. (Joshua 1:7)

SPOILER ALERT: These words were spoken by God through Joshua to God's special people *after they had been saved from Egyptian slavery.* And yes, Miriam has a lot to do with that. You see, she is one important part of a Bible story that's probably familiar to you. What story? The one about Moses and the Exodus of God's people from Egypt! The verse above are the words God spoke long after they'd left their slavery, and it was finally time for them to go into a special piece of land that they called the Promised Land.

Based on Joshua 1:7, write the three things that God instructed the people of Israel to "be" as they went to the Promised Land.

1. God told the people to be strong
2. he told them to be courageous
3. he told them to not deviate

It probably doesn't surprise you that God's people had to be strong to live courageous lives. But what did you think when you read that they also needed to be careful to obey? When God tells someone in the Bible to be courageous, it often comes with this encouragement to be obedient.

But, for God's people, there was one problem . . . the land was full of giants! (Think Goliath-sized guys!) Yikes! *Who wouldn't be afraid of people like that?*

Courage requires obedience because, otherwise, we might chicken out. It looks more like faithful obedience to God than doing extraordinary things. If you want to be a girl of courage, start small. Choose to obey God in the little things, no matter how hard it may be.

THE TRUTH: Courage is <u>living</u> in <u>faithful</u> <u>obedience</u>.

Who knows? Those little acts of faithful obedience may just turn into something extraordinary!

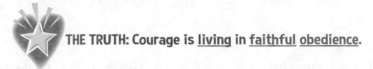

Grab your megaphone of Truth!

I spy a lie! Cross out the lie below and fill in the blank by writing the truth!

LIE: Courage is doing something extraordinary.

TRUTH: Courage is ___living___ in ___faithful obedience___ .

LIE #2: Courage Is Something Some People Are Born With.

When we see someone do courageous things, we are only seeing a little snapshot of their lives. Maybe you know a firefighter who rescued a child from a burning building. (That sounds courageous!) Or perhaps you have seen someone in your school stand up to a bully. (That's super brave!) It could even be that you have met my daughter Autumn. (She's my inspiration for courage!)

But when you hear about their courageous moment, you don't see all the moments that lead up to it. You don't see how they *learned* to be brave. You see, courage is learned over time as you watch others who are even more courageous than you!

Think back to who you wrote down as the most courageous person you know. What are some things you can learn from them?

 I learned that if I ever get a cast I should be corageous like Ansley.

Start there! Practice those habits, qualities, and behaviors. When you do, you'll be in training to be a girl of courage.

One thing that trains us to be brave is to study how Jesus lived and learn to be more like Him. After all, He was courageous enough to die for us! He also stood up for people who others treated badly and hung out with people who were not popular. As you imitate Jesus and others, you begin setting an example for everyone else who comes after you. Don't believe me?

Check out this verse. Use your favorite color to underline the word in it that describes you.

> Don't let anyone think less of you because you are young. Be an example to all believers in what you say, in the way you live, in your love, your faith, and your purity. (1 Timothy 4:12)

People can learn from you even though you are young. Set an example not just in love, faith, and purity, but in courage!

THE TRUTH: Courage is a character quality you learn from Jesus and others who love Him.

I don't know about you, but I sure wasn't born courageous. And I'm still learning. It's OK if you are, too!

Grab your megaphone of Truth!

I spy a lie! Cross out the lie below and fill in the blank by writing the truth!

LIE: Courage is something *some* people are born with.

TRUTH: Courage is a *character* *quality* you *learn* from *Jesus* and others who *love* *him*.

Lie #3: Courage is something you feel.

In movies, courage is often presented as this magical moment of truth where the *feeling* of courage wells up inside a person before they go and do something heroic. But that's not how courage works at all. Courage is a choice to take action in spite of what you feel! And I don't know about you, but I often feel very afraid when I most need to be courageous.

In the space below, write about a time when you have felt afraid, but needed to have courage.

I was afraid to do a cartweel on the beam but I did it anyway.

It's OK to be afraid. It's normal.

Do you remember those big giants I told you about? They made the Israelites feel fear, and lots of it! But check out these instructions God gave to them. (This may sound familiar, but it's a different verse than the one we looked at earlier.)

> So be strong and courageous! Do not be afraid and do not panic before them. For the LORD your God will personally go ahead of you. He will neither fail you nor abandon you. (Deuteronomy 31:6)

NOTE: Fear is not always bad. For example, if you're walking on a trail in a forest and you see a bear, fear will help you make a wise choice. (Hopefully, you'll walk the other way and stay a safe distance.) It can be difficult to know when fear is telling you useful information or just holding you back. So, promise me when you feel afraid you will tell an adult you trust!

The Israelites felt fear. That was their *feeling*. But God invited them to choose courage. And to be strong.

Look back at the verse and cross out the words "afraid" and "panic."

That's what we want to do in life. We want to live in such a way that we cancel fear that holds us back and live in courage. So, you can't listen to your feelings when they disagree with God's Word. The Israelites didn't need to listen to their feelings because God promised to go ahead of them. Better yet, He promised "not" to do two things.

What did God say He would not do?

> God promised to not fail or abandon the Israelites

Courage is choosing to trust God when you feel afraid. He will not leave you or fail you. Not only do you have to choose to believe that He will help you overcome your fear, but you also need to trust Him for the outcome.

THE TRUTH: Courage is a choice to trust God.

Courage is not the absence of feelings, but a *choice* we make to trust God.

Grab your megaphone of Truth!

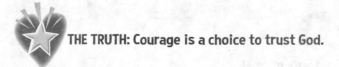

I spy a lie! Cross out the lie below and fill in the blank by writing the truth!

~~LIE: Courage is something you feel.~~

TRUTH: Courage is a __choice__ to __trust__ __God__.

Lie #4: Courage comes from inside you.

The world will constantly tell you that *you* are the source of your strength. *"Look inside yourself!"* people say. *"Courage comes from inside!"*

Well, I'm here to tell you that courage does *not* come from you. God *alone* is your strength. He is the one who gives you courage!

Let's look at a chapter we will dive into later in our study, Exodus 15. The Israelites had just escaped slavery in Egypt and crossed the Red Sea. (If you don't know that story yet, don't worry because as I mentioned we'll read all about it later.) When they made it safely to the other shore, the waters came crashing down, destroying Pharaoh and his army who were following close behind. God's people looked back and they knew something for certain about courage: where it came from. In fact, they sang about it in a special song.

 The Lord is my strength and my song;
he has given me victory. (Exodus 15:2a)

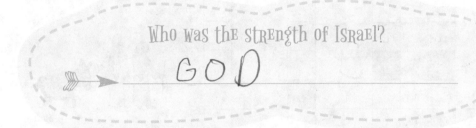

Who was the strength of Israel?

➤ ___GOD_____

God was their strength in times of trouble. Because of the power of God, they had the courage to leave Egypt so that they could start a new life in the Promised Land!

 **THE TRUTH: Courage comes from God.**

Courage does not come from within. Courage comes from God—the only source of strength!

Grab your megaphone of Truth! ((📢

I spy a lie! Cross out the lie below and fill in the blank by writing the truth!

~~LIE: Courage comes from inside you.~~

TRUTH: Courage comes from ___GOD___.

THE GOOD & THE BAD ISRAELITES

Using the clues below, fill in four of the good and courageous choices the Israelites made. Then, fill in four of the sins and some of the mistakes they made while traveling in the wilderness. (Hint: Spaces are included in color.) If you need to, look up the Bible verses to find the word!

Crossword puzzle with answers:
1 Down: FIRE, then AND, then CLOUD
2 Down: RED SEA

UP AND DOWN:
Good and Courageous Choices

1. Followed the pillars of *Cloud & fire* faithfully. (Exodus 13:21–22)

2. Crossed the *RED SEA*. (Exodus 14:21)

3. _____ ____ _____ were confident in the Promised Land. (Numbers 14:6–9)

4. Marched around _____. (Joshua 6)

LEFT TO RIGHT:
Sins and Mistakes

5. Failing to trust God to enter the _____ _____. (Numbers 14:1–4)

6. Complaining over the lack of _____. (Exodus 17:2–3)

7. Building and worshiping the _____ _____. (Exodus 32:7–10)

8. Attempting to collect _____ on the Sabbath. (Exodus 16:27–29)

For puzzle answers, go to page 110.

Lie #5: Courageous people never make mistakes.

In a fairy-tale world, the hero of the story is often portrayed as the perfect example of goodness. And . . . they never make mistakes. Everyone praises them for their bravery and courage as they fight for the good of all.

Sadly, we don't live in a fairy-tale world.

We are all broken people and every one of us makes mistakes. In fact, not only do we do things by accident, but we also sin. Romans 3:23 reminds us that "everyone has sinned."

But do you know who was courageous? The Israelites! Every single one of them left the world they knew to enter the land the Lord was taking them to. (Hey, that reminds me of my daughter Autumn!)

You know who *also* made a lot of mistakes? The Israelites! They disobeyed God and cowered in fear time and time again. As we study Miriam's story, you'll learn that even though God was faithful to the Israelites, they were not always faithful to God.

Just like that puzzle on the previous page, the Israelites were a mixture of courageous choices and sinful choices. But there's good news. Here's what one of the Israelites wrote about how God responded to their bad decisions.

> Where is another God like you, who pardons the guilt of the remnant, overlooking the sins of his special people? You will not stay angry with your people forever, because you delight in showing unfailing love. (Micah 7:18)

God did not stay angry when the Israelites sinned, but instead He showed unfailing love to them even when they made mistakes. Some versions of the Bible use the word *mercy* to describe what God gave the Israelites. If that's a new word for you, here's a definition that might help.

 { **Mercy: love and compassion for someone who does not deserve it.** }

We all make mistakes. We all sin. And we all need *mercy*, even courageous people!

 THE TRUTH: Courageous people need God's mercy, too.

I want you to hear this *really* loud and clear so I'm gonna put it in great big letters:

God loves you! He loves you when you are good. And He loves you when you are bad.

Even though there are often consequences when you sin, He will never stop showing you kindness and love. (Consequences are the good things or the bad things that happen as a result of our actions and decisions!)

Once when I was asking some tween girls if God loved them, they all said "yes." But then I started talking about their sin and many felt like God didn't love them when they were bad. That makes me really sad because it's a lie. **The truth is that God loves you all the time, no matter what!**

Grab your megaphone of Truth!

I spy a lie! Cross out the lie below and fill in the blank by writing the truth!

LIE: Courageous people never make mistakes.

TRUTH: Courageous people need _____ _____, too.

Whew! Zooming is hard work. Now get ready to zero in!

ZERO IN: What does it mean?

So, what does everything we just studied mean for you? Does it mean you need to pick up and move and look for a promised land and hope there are no giants there?

No! But what you just learned really is useful for your life today. First, let's review. **What are the five truths about courage?**

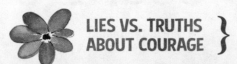

LIES VS. TRUTHS ABOUT COURAGE }

Draw a line from each **lie** we sometimes believe about courage to the **truth** that replaces it.

LIES

1. Courage is doing something extraordinary.

2. Courage is something some people are born with.

3. Courage is something you feel.

4. Courage comes from inside you.

5. Courageous people never make mistakes.

TRUTHS

 1. Courage is a character quality you learn from Jesus and others who love Him.

 2. Courageous people need God's mercy, too.

 3. Courage is a choice to trust God.

 4. Courage is living in faithful obedience.

 5. Courage comes from God.

For puzzle answers, go to page 110.

What Courage Is

The five truths we learned about courage can be summed up like this: *Courage is doing the right thing even when it's hard or you are afraid.*

There's a verse that reminds me of this definition.

 The wicked flee when no one pursues, but the righteous are bold as a lion. (Proverbs 28:1 ESV)

Everyone is afraid sometimes, but people who don't trust in God can get so scared they run even when they don't need to! But when you are doing the right thing—that is to say, when you are righteous—you are bold like a lion!

Courage

▶ Fill in the blank!

Courage is _____ _____ _____ _____

even when it's _____ or you are _____.

Go back to your Courage Lessons at the beginning of this study and write that important definition of courage there.

We can be courageous every single day of our lives because each day we have choices to make. Will you choose to trust God and do the right thing? Or will you choose to listen to your feelings?

ZIP IT UP: What does God want me to do with it?

OK, let's zip it up for today. It's time to respond to God. End your study time by talking to Him about what you've learned. In your journal entry below, you might start by telling God about something that frightens you. Then, ask Him to make you courageous!

_____

_____

_____

_____

_____

_____

_____

_____

_____

_____

_____

Becoming a girl of courage is not an easy task. But just like the Israelites had to learn how to be courageous, you can learn to be courageous too! One of those Israelites who chose courage in the face of danger was Miriam—a girl just like you! And since we often learn best by example, we will study the life of this courageous girl from the Bible.

Sometimes when we are studying the Bible, it's helpful to take notes and keep them all in the same place. That way you can look back later and see themes that run throughout the whole story. At the beginning of this study, I created special pages for your notes on the life of Miriam. You probably saw these pages when you first opened this book.

Turn to page 7. You'll see the five main characters in the life of Miriam. Write their names under their pictures to help you remember who they are!

⭐ **Miriam**—She's the biggest one in the center labeled *A Prophetess*.

⭐ **Moses & Aaron**—These are Miriam's brothers. They're the two guys to the left of Miriam.

⭐ **Mom & Dad**—Their real names are Amram and Jochebed, but to keep it simple, you could just label them Mom and Dad! You'll find their picture to the right of Miriam.

✳ A Courageous Girl Is Obedient

Have you ever had to be courageous at a sleepover? I'm not talking about the kind of courage you need when it gets dark, you're the only one who can't sleep, and the ticking clock strikes terror into your very being! I mean the kind of courage you need when your friends decide to watch a movie you know your parents don't want you to see. Maybe you wonder: *Should I go with the flow and watch the movie, or obey my parents and speak up?*

Like it or not, everyone faces times when they have to stand up for what they know is right. Sometimes courage looks like saying no to watching a movie at a sleepover. Or it's standing up for someone who's being bullied by mean girls.

For Miriam, courage meant babysitting her little brother! Now you may be thinking, "What does courage have to do with watching a baby?" Well, you're about to find out! **It's time to start zooming!**

ZOOM

Zoom In & Out—Who? What? Where? When? Why?

To help us understand Miriam's courage, we need to zoom out to see what was happening hundreds of years before she was even born in Egypt. It was even before her mom and dad were born slaves. You see, the Israelites weren't always captive to Pharaoh.

Let's go back to meet one of the very first Israelites who became a slave in Egypt. His name was Joseph. (If you don't know his story, you can read about it in Genesis 37 and 39–45.) When Joseph's older brothers got super jealous of him, they sold him to be a slave. (For the record, that's a super bad thing to do and not a great way to solve jealousy!) Joseph's new owners took him from his home in Canaan to Egypt.

Fast-forward a whole bunch, and God gave Joseph the ability to interpret one of Pharaoh's dreams. Isn't that so cool?! This dream told him that Egypt would have seven *good* years of harvest when the land would have lots of food. But then they would have seven *bad* years of famine when there would be no food at all.

Pharaoh believed it and got busy storing up food during the good years. He even put Joseph in charge of sharing that food with people during the bad years! That's when—through a lot of twists and turns—Joseph's family came to Egypt. You might guess this, but they were very hungry! Joseph forgave them and fed them and said something like, "Hey, why don't you move here to live near me?"

And they did!

Over the years, Joseph's family grew bigger and bigger.

In the meantime, Joseph died. And so did the Pharaoh who liked and respected him.

Now, since we're zooming . . . let's travel through time a few hundred years to the days when Miriam was probably a baby.

The new Pharaoh who was ruling in Egypt didn't remember the story of Joseph helping his nation. He saw the Israelites, who were also called the Hebrews, as a problem rather than a blessing. Because there were so many of them, he was afraid that they would try to take over his country. Here's where we should probably dig into our Bibles to learn some really important things.

Use a dark pencil to underline the evil words the Pharaoh spoke to the midwives. (That's what you call a woman who helps other women when they have their babies!)

Then Pharaoh, the king of Egypt, gave this order to the Hebrew midwives, Shiphrah and Puah: "When you help the Hebrew women as they give birth, watch as they deliver. If the baby is a boy, kill him; if it is a girl, let her live." But because the midwives feared God, they refused to obey the king's orders. They allowed the boys to live, too. (Exodus 1:15–17)

How awful! The new Pharaoh was one bad guy. But the midwives were COURAGEOUS! They didn't listen to Pharaoh because they knew God wouldn't want them to do such an evil thing! Children are a blessing from God, not a threat.

Now wait a minute! Didn't we *just* talk about how courage means living in faithful *obedience*? But the midwives were *disobeying* Pharaoh! Something doesn't quite add up. Let's dig into this a little.

In Acts 5, you can read a story about some people who faced the decision to either obey an earthly authority or obey God. Read what Peter, one of the twelve men personally trained by Jesus, said in the verse below.

Circle the one authority we must always obey.

Peter and the apostles replied, "We must obey God rather than any human authority." (Acts 5:29)

If someone who has authority here on earth asks us to disobey God, we shouldn't do it. The Hebrew midwives obeyed God by disobeying that evil Pharaoh.

Well, when Pharaoh couldn't get the midwives to do his dirty work for him, he hatched another evil plan to get rid of all the baby boys.

Use your dark pencil again to underline his new instructions.

 Then Pharaoh gave this order to all his people: "Throw every newborn Hebrew boy into the Nile River. But you may let the girls live." (Exodus 1:22)

Use a blue pencil to draw wavy water lines under the words that reveal the exact place where Pharaoh hoped the baby boys of Israel would die.

If the Hebrew midwives wouldn't kill the babies when they were born, Pharaoh hoped that his own people, the Egyptians, would drown their slaves' babies in the Nile River.

Well, I don't know about you, but I'm thinking the Israelite people needed a hero! Guess what? One was about to show up, but she wouldn't have a superhero cape or a cool gadget. Why she wouldn't even be an adult, but a tween girl—just like you.

ZOOM IN

Now that you have some *context*, it's time to start learning about courage from Miriam's example. There's just one problem. Her name doesn't even show up the first time we read about her in the Bible.

EXODUS 2:1-6

As you read, use a yellow pencil to circle the words "baby's sister" or "Pharaoh's daughter" every time they appear in this passage.

1 About this time, a man and woman from the tribe of Levi got married. 2 The woman became pregnant and gave birth to a son. She saw that he was a special baby and kept him hidden for three months. 3 But when she could no longer hide him, she got a basket made of papyrus reeds and waterproofed it with tar and pitch.

She put the baby in the basket and laid it among the reeds along the bank of the Nile River.

4 The baby's sister then stood at a distance, watching to see what would happen to him.

5 Soon Pharaoh's daughter came down to bathe in the river, and her attendants walked along

the riverbank. When the princess saw the basket among the reeds, she sent her maid to get it for

her. 6 When the princess opened it, she saw the baby. The little boy was crying, and she felt sorry

for him. "This must be one of the Hebrew children," she said.

**Who is this passage about? Using the clues below, write the names or titles of the
four main characters below.**

♥ _____

She must have been good at making baskets.

♥ _____

The tween girl "stood at a distance."

♥ _____

Pharaoh didn't want this one to live.

♥ _____

She discovered something surprising when she took a bath!

**In the passage, circle the names of anyone in that list who you think was acting
courageously. Write below why you think their actions were courageous.**

_____

_____

_____

_____

The baby, who was later named **Moses**, was at great risk! Any old Egyptian who found him was legally allowed to take him into the Nile River and drown him. So, his **mom** built a basket to hide him but couldn't stay to watch the baby nap. Big sis **Miriam** stuck around and saw **Pharaoh's daughter** discover her brother! Talk about a nail-biter! Let's zoom in to understand more about what happened.

Circle the language that this part of the Bible was originally written in. (Look back at the Introduction if you need help.)

english ♥ Swahili ♥ Hebrew ♥ Pig Latin

In the original language of Hebrew, the word for basket has much more meaning. When Moses's mom could no longer hide him, she put the baby in a *tevah* and laid it among the reeds along the bank of the Nile River.

> **⋯▶** { **tevah**: the Hebrew word for an oblong boat or an ark. }

Hold the phone! Do you see what I see? Let me help you in case you don't.
Can you guess what other story from the Bible uses the word **tevah**?

The Story of Adam and Eve
The Story of Noah ♥ The story of Lazarus

If you circled **The Story of Noah**, you're correct. God used Noah's ark to save one family and all the animals from a global flood. And God was about to use a much smaller ark to hide a baby who God would use to save the next generation of a nation from slavery.

Where did Moses's mother place that ark-basket? And why is that kind of hard to believe based on what Pharaoh has told the Egyptians to do?

⟫⟫➤ _____

_____

_____

_____

_____

Moses's mom must have had a lot of faith. She literally put the baby in the exact spot where Pharaoh hoped all of the Hebrew babies would be killed. I'm pretty sure that it had more than goldfish in it. (Think: crocodiles!) This mother didn't hide her baby far, far away from the Nile River, but right inside of it. Can you imagine!?

Well, she may have been the one to put her baby into that ark-basket, but she wasn't the one who stayed to watch it. Maybe she had work to do. (She *was*, after all, a slave.) So she assigned that task to Miriam, the tween girl who "stood at a distance" to watch the basket.

What is the main thing that Miriam was doing in this passage of Scripture?
(Hint: What do we call it when an older sister watches her baby brother or sister?)

_____

_____

Who do you think asked her to do this? In other words, who was she obeying?

_____

_____

Why do you think Miriam stood at a distance?

_____

_____

Maybe she stood at a distance when she was babysitting Moses so she wouldn't attract attention to the spot where the ark-basket was hiding. But I'm pretty sure Miriam was also afraid. I would be! But she didn't let fear stop her from obeying her mother's request to babysit her brother. (Remember, courage is not the absence of fear. It's obeying God and doing the right thing *even when* you feel afraid.)

If you can believe it, babysitting Moses in the very spot where Pharaoh wanted him to die was just the beginning of Miriam's courage.

EXODUS 2:7–10

Let's keep reading the story of Miriam and baby Moses. Underline the courageous action you see in the verses below.

7 Then the baby's sister approached the princess. "Should I go and find one of the Hebrew women to nurse the baby for you?" she asked. **8** "Yes, do!" the princess replied. So the girl went and called the baby's mother. **9** "Take this baby and nurse him for me," the princess told the baby's mother. "I will pay you for your help." So the woman took her baby home and nursed him. **10** Later, when the boy was older, his mother brought him back to Pharaoh's daughter, who adopted him as her own son. The princess named him Moses, for she explained, "I lifted him out of the water."

Wow! Miriam and her mom *both* had a lot of courage, didn't they? They risked their lives in order to protect baby Moses! You probably underlined a lot of courageous acts, but let's check your work.

COURAGE BY THE NILE } Circle all of the courageous things Miriam and her mom did in today's Bible reading.

MIRIAM'S MOM PLACED MOSES IN THE NILE RIVER.

Miriam ran away when she saw Pharaoh's daughter.

Miriam's mom hid baby Moses.

Miriam fed the crocodiles.

miriam spoke up.

Miriam found a houseboat to hang out in.

MIRIAM WATCHED HER BABY BROTHER IN THE WATER.

Miriam's mom made an ark-basket.

For puzzle answers, go to page 110.

Miriam sure was a shero! (That's what I sometimes call it when a girl is the hero!) Who knows what would have happened to her baby brother if she hadn't been willing to babysit and think quickly when the Pharaoh's daughter showed up. But the fact is, she really didn't do anything extraordinary. She was simply living in faithful obedience to God and to her mom. Here's where we can see **COURAGE LESSON #1: A courageous girl lives in faithful obedience.**

Fill in the blank!
Courage Lesson #1:

A courageous girl lives in

_____   _____

Go back to your **Courage Lessons** page at the beginning of this study.
Beside #1, rewrite the sentence above.

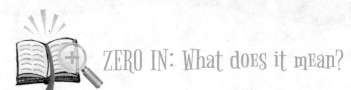

ZERO IN: What does it mean?

Now, what do all of these verses mean for you and me? What does courage look like in our everyday lives? Well, just like Miriam, we need to live in faithful obedience. This means that we need to obey God and do the things He calls us to do no matter what.

Has there ever been a time in your life when it took courage to obey God? Write about a memory you have where you acted with courage by living in faithful obedience.

If you're not really sure, it's OK. Obeying God takes a long time to learn because you have to be able to understand what He wants from you. Thankfully, He has given us someone to help us practice.

In the verse below, circle who can help us learn obedience.

 Children, obey your parents because you belong to the Lord, for this is the right thing to do. (Ephesians 6:1)

If you obey your parents and other authorities in your life like teachers or grandparents, you can be sure that God will be pleased! It is one way that you can obey Him. And, as they teach you, you learn about other ways to be courageous.

IN MY OWN LIFE

On a scale of 1 to 10, how often are you obedient?

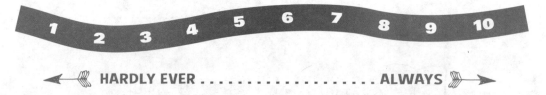

1 2 3 4 5 6 7 8 9 10

◄── HARDLY EVER . . . . ALWAYS ──►

Using the pairs of words below, circle the one that most often describes how you obey.

Immediately . . . . OR . . . . Eventually

With a happy heart . . . . OR . . . . With a grumbling heart

The words on the left describe how we *should* obey! When you act immediately and with a happy heart, you have obeyed. (And it's extra awesome when you know what your parents want you to do—like make your bed—and you do it without them telling you to.)

The words on the right describe ways we *technically* obey, but our hearts haven't really fully participated. I'm not sure you can even call delayed, grumbling actions obedience.

Based on how you describe your obedience, do you need to make some changes about how you respond to authority in your life?

 _____

Do you remember our definition for courage? Courage is doing the right thing even when it is hard or you are afraid. Sometimes obeying God or others, like Mom and Dad, is difficult. But the right thing to do is to obey immediately with a happy heart.

ZIP IT UP: What does God want me to do with it?

Choosing to be obedient is not always easy. (That's why we sometimes need to do it courageously.) If you didn't come out too well on the obedience scale, ask God for help. You could even ask your mom or dad for forgiveness. Make today a fresh start. In your journal entry below, write a prayer confessing any areas of disobedience in your life, and asking God for the courage to live in faithful obedience!

_____

_____

_____

_____

_____

_____

_____

_____

_____

_____

Turn to the page at the beginning of this study where you're keeping notes on Miriam. Write down anything you learned about her.

Congratulations! You've just finished the first courage lesson in our study of the life of Miriam! I'm so proud of you! You are living in faithful obedience to God as you seek to learn more about His Word.

Be sure to join me for the next lesson soon.

✳ A Courageous Girl Learns from Godly People

Don't you just love *first-time evers*? There's the first-time ever that you go to the movie theater or ride a horse or solve an algebra equation. We all have first-time evers. And in some ways, they are really great. They're fun, and we have something awesome to tell people. "I did it!" we say happily.

But first-time evers are also really scary! I remember my first-time ever to snorkel. Wow! I was so excited. And super afraid. *What if I couldn't breathe through that tube thingy? What if the waves were too high for me when I came up for air? What if my goggles fogged up and I couldn't see?* I needed help to get over my fear. It took courage to get in the water and to stay in the water.

You might be facing some first-time evers soon. Guess what? I know just what you need to find your courage.

But before you zoom off and discover what that is, let's remember what we learned last time. **Look back at your Courage Lessons page at the beginning of this study. Write the first one below.**

⋯⋯► **Fill in the blank!**

★ **COURAGE LESSON #1**

A courageous girl lives in _____

_____.

OK. Let's learn Courage Lesson #2.

► **Zoom In & Out—Who? What? Where? When? Why?**

When we left Miriam, she had just courageously babysat her brother Moses while he slept in an ark-basket. (That's no big deal if your parents are at the movies, but it's super dangerous if Pharaoh wants to kill all the Hebrew boys in Egypt.) Miriam also had the courage to speak up when Pharaoh's daughter came looking for a relaxing bath in the Nile River and discovered that sweet baby boy. His big sis jumped into action and told that princess about someone she knew—her mom—who could help her raise the baby until it was older.

And that, my friend, was how baby Moses was saved!

That sure took a lot of courage!

Was Miriam born bold, or did she take an extra-credit class in courage? Let's dig for the answer. You actually can't find it in any of the verses in the Old Testament that talk about Miriam. But it does exist.

Let's zoom waaaay out again to learn who taught Miriam to be courageous. We'll discover the answer in the New Testament book of Hebrews.

HEBREWS 11:23–29

Read just verse 23 for now and underline the entire verse with your favorite color.

23 It was by faith that Moses' parents hid him for three months when he was born. They saw that God had given them an unusual child, and they were not afraid to disobey the king's command. 24 It was by faith that Moses, when he grew up, refused to be called the son of Pharaoh's daughter. 25 He chose to share the oppression of God's people instead of enjoying the fleeting pleasures of sin. 26 He thought it was better to suffer for the sake of Christ than to own the treasures of Egypt, for he was looking ahead to his great reward. 27 It was by faith that Moses left the land of Egypt, not fearing the king's anger. He kept right on going because he kept his eyes on the one who is invisible. 28 It was by faith that Moses commanded the people of Israel to keep the Passover and to sprinkle blood on the doorposts so that the angel of death would not kill their firstborn sons. 29 It was by faith that the people of Israel went right through the Red Sea as though they were on dry ground. But when the Egyptians tried to follow, they were all drowned.

Who does this verse say gets credit for saving baby Moses?

 _____

Poor Miriam. She didn't get credit. It was Moses's parents, right? (And, of course, they just so happened to be Miriam's parents too!)

What does it say they did to save their baby boy? And for how long did they do it?

 _____

_____

Why did they do it? (Hint: What could they see about the baby?)

_____

_____

OK, here's a really hard one. Who do you think was watching them do that? (Hint: Her name isn't in this piece of Scripture either.)

_____

SPOILER ALERT: You might already know this, but Moses grew up to be courageous, too. God raised him up as the leader of Israel! He used Moses to rescue His special people from slavery and to lead the Israelites toward the Promised Land. But, in the verses that we'll study today, that is all hundreds of years in the past!

Miriam learned courage from her parents! You may recall that their names were Jochebed and Amram. First, they bravely hid their son. Then Moses's mom built an ark-basket to hide him in the Nile River. And someone was watching: Miriam. Their tween daughter's eyes were on them. She was in their unofficial school of courage!

And the amazing thing is that Jochebed and Amram are still teaching tween girls by their example. (They just taught you!) And it's not just courage that they teach with their lives. They are just two of the many examples of _faith_ we read about in Hebrews 11.

Let's keep reading Hebrews 11. Starting in verse 24, go back and read the rest of today's key Bible verses and circle anything courageous that Moses did.

Oh, how I wish we had time to study all of Moses's courageous actions. And let me tell you, few people struggled with fear like this guy! If anyone proves you can have courage, even if you are afraid, it's Moses. God put him in charge of an entire nation, and he (with help from his brother and right-hand man, Aaron) stood up to Pharaoh on God's behalf and said, "Let my people go!" They led the Israelite people out of Egypt. That took a lot of courage! But we're not here to learn about them. We're here to learn about Miriam! So let me ask you a difficult question.

THE COURAGE OF MOSES

Use the key below to decode and finish the sentences describing Moses's courageous acts!

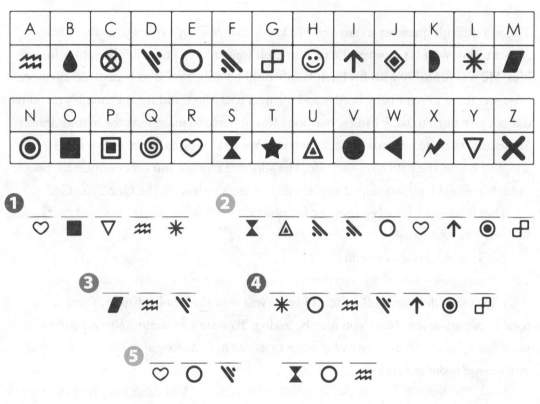

Moses's courageous acts included these obedient choices:

1 Giving up his position in the _____ family (Heb. 11:24)

2 _____ as a slave in Egypt (Heb. 11:25)

3 Leaving Egypt even though it made Pharaoh _____ (Heb. 11:27)

4 _____ the people of Israel to overcome death (Heb. 11:28)

5 Crossing the _____ _____ (Heb. 11:29)

For puzzle answers, go to page 110.

Did you get all of them? If not, go back through the verses above and underline what you missed.

Who do you think taught Moses to be courageous? (There's not really a correct answer. Just give it your best guess.)

This is a difficult question to answer! We know that Miriam's courage enabled baby Moses to live with his mom and dad a little bit longer after Pharaoh's daughter found him. He was probably with his birth family until he didn't need to breastfeed anymore. (You see, there weren't baby bottles and formula back then, and since Pharaoh's daughter did not give birth to baby Moses, her body was not able to make milk for him to drink.) Sometime when he was two or so, he would have left his birth home to live in his adoptive home, the palace on the Nile. His adoptive mother and other important people in his life would have worshiped any number of idols instead of the One True God.

That leaves us with a big mystery to solve: Who modeled faith in God and courage to obey Him for Moses?

Let's consider one possibility.

Go back to today's verses from Hebrews. Circle every time the word **faith** shows up!

How many did you find? I found five. If you read the whole chapter, there are a total of twenty-seven. Now, you may be asking: *Why are we counting how many times the word "faith" is used in Hebrews 11 if we're supposed to be talking about the courage of a girl we read about in Exodus?*

Well, it's because faith is the foundation for courage! You can't have true courage without faith in God. Without faith, we would be overwhelmed by our fears. Trusting that God is in control gives us the ability to live courageously! But for now, let's just remember that Jochebed and Amram, Miriam's parents, were special examples of faith in God. That's why we're reading about them in this very special chapter about faith thousands of years after they lived.

Because of their great faith, I'm sure they prayed God would plant true faith and bravery into their son even though he was growing up in a palace that worshiped other gods! God answered the prayers of two special parents. By the time Moses was a whopping 40 years old, he had realized that he didn't belong in Pharaoh's house and that he was an Israelite by birth. Not only that, but he left his position as a prince to become a poor laborer among the Israelites. Imagine leaving all the wealth and privilege of the royal palace to go be a slave! Well, that's what Moses chose.

I don't know who actually taught Moses courage, but someone did. Perhaps it was God Himself. We don't know if God spoke to Moses when he was a boy, but we do know that He spoke to him when he was an adult. The way God spoke to Moses was very special. It was direct. Moses is one of a handful of people God spoke to in the Old Testament who are called *prophets*. Perhaps it was the prayers of Jochebed and Amram for their baby boy that moved God to speak so openly to Moses. That's the kind of impossible thing God does when we have faith in Him.

One thing is for sure: No one is just born courageous. We are trained by God or others who love Him to live faith-filled, brave lives.

Here's COURAGE LESSON #2: A courageous girl has learned that character quality from Jesus and others who love Him.

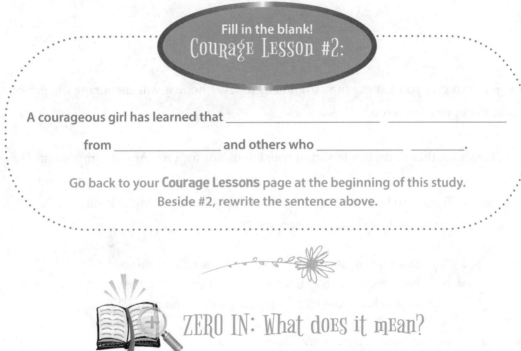

Fill in the blank!
COURAGE LESSON #2:

A courageous girl has learned that _____ _____

from _____ and others who _____ _____.

Go back to your **Courage Lessons** page at the beginning of this study.
Beside #2, rewrite the sentence above.

ZERO IN: What does it mean?

Phew! All of that zooming was hard work. Now it's time to zero in! What does all of this stuff have to do with you?

Well, to begin with, you need to find courageous women to learn from. Just like Miriam followed the example provided by her parents, you should follow the example of others who are living courageously by following Jesus. In the New Testament, the apostle Paul wrote this simple instruction down for Christians.

Circle the word that shows up two times.

And you should imitate me, just as I imitate Christ.
(1 Corinthians 11:1)

To imitate someone is to copy them. That's what Miriam did. She copied her mom's courage. And her mom, Jochebed, was getting courage from God. YOU and I need to do the same thing. We need to imitate the courage of women who copy Jesus' life and behavior *and* courage.

IN MY OWN LIFE

Who do you know that has great faith and lives courageously because of it?

_____

_____

_____

I'm going to give you a super fun assignment today. I hope it will encourage the person whose name you just wrote.

But first . . .

There's another thing this lesson in courage means for you. And it's important. *You are teaching girls younger than you by the way you choose to live.* If you're courageous, those girls will learn to be brave. If you're fearful, you'll be passing that on.

Do you remember this verse from chapter 1?

 Don't let anyone think less of you because you are young.
Be an example to all believers in what you say, in the way you live,
in your love, your faith, and your purity. (1 Timothy 4:12)

What does this mean for you if you are a believer in God?

_____

_____

Who do you think is watching your life to copy your behavior?

_____

_____

Are you a good example of faith and courage? Why or why not?

_____

_____

_____

♥ **Fill in Your Heart!**

How does all of this make you feel? Do you think you're a good example of courage and faith? Who do you know that is a courageous, faith-filled person that you look up to? **As you write, take time to thank the Lord for those people!**

ZIP IT UP: What does God want me to do with it?

Time to zip it up! Since this chapter is all about the importance of becoming courageous by following the example of others, I want you to do two things.

First, think about someone in your life who may look up to you as an example. (Maybe it's a younger sibling or a friend!) In today's journal entry, write a prayer asking God to help you set an example of courage for them.

_____

_____

_____

_____

_____

Second, grab a notecard or some paper. The funkier the better! Write a note to the person you look up to. Tell them they are a great example of courage. Maybe include a sentence or two on what you have learned from them and thank them for being a good model. When you're finished, deliver the note to them!

_____

_____

_____

_____

_____

OK, it's time to turn to the page with your notes on Miriam at the beginning of the study and record what you've learned about her mom and dad! I sure would like to meet them. They sound amazing! Write down anything interesting that you want to remember.

And before you close this book for the day, let me ask you something. Do you understand what it means to have faith in Jesus Christ? It might be a good time to be sure you do. Go to the pages at the back of this study if you want to learn more.

If you do have faith in Jesus, consider praying for someone you know who does not. Some people who don't know Him become overwhelmed with fear. Without faith, it's really hard for them to have courage when times are tough.

Think about someone you know who doesn't know Jesus as their Lord and Savior. Write their name in the blank below. Commit to pray for them every day this week using this prayer or by writing one of your own!

JESUS, PLEASE HELP

_____

to come to know You as their Lord and Savior. Soften their heart and show them how to put their faith in You. Give them courage to face the hard things in life and show them that hope can only be found in You!

In Jesus' name, Amen!

CHAPTER 4

✳ A Courageous Girl Chooses to Trust God

Imagine you're going to jump off a high dive. It's your first time ever. You climb up and up and up, and then you crawl out to the edge of the board. Everything looks so very far away from up there.

"Just jump!" your friends holler from one side of the pool.

You look back at the ladder and think, "Maybe I should just climb back down."

"You have to jump or let someone else take a turn," says the lifeguard.

You're just so afraid!

But then, you look to the other side of the pool, and there's your mom. She's sitting back comfortably enjoying the sun as she patiently waits for you to tackle your first-time ever on the high dive! She smiles sweetly and confidently at you as if to say, "You *can* do this!" And that's when you realize everything is going to be fine.

How do you know? **Because you can trust your mom!**

You push, despite your fear, and make a decision: *It's time to jump!*

Splash!

The high dive isn't too scary after all!

Miriam didn't jump off the high dive, but that may have been easier than babysitting her baby brother by the Nile River. She guarded him while he slept in an ark-basket and protected him when he was discovered by Pharaoh's daughter. That was courageous. Let's review our big definition for that important word. (If you need help, look back at chapter 1.)

► Fill in the blank!

Courage is doing the _____ _____

even when it's hard or you are afraid.

So far, we've learned two important lessons about being brave. Go back to your Courage Lessons page at the beginning of the study and write them below.

⭐ **COURAGE LESSON #1** _____

_____

⭐ **COURAGE LESSON #2** _____

_____

_____

It's time to discover Courage Lesson #3.

► Zoom In & Out—Who? What? Where? When? Why?

A lot of time has passed since Moses was a baby. He's now old enough to be your dad! And, as we learned in the last chapter, he left the royal palace to live among the Israelites. He knew he was one of them.

But living among the slaves was horrible because the Egyptians treated them so badly. In fact, Moses actually saw an Egyptian soldier beating an Israelite for not working hard enough.

Moses just couldn't take it!

He did something really bad. And then he ran away to live in the desert and be a shepherd.

Wait . . . what!?

Isn't God supposed to use him to rescue His special people? You mean Moses left them back in Egypt?

Yes. Yes, he did.

If you read the story of Moses, you'll learn that he probably felt a lot of bad, super-sticky emotions, including fear. That's why he ran away! And this is precisely where we'll pick up Miriam's story today. It's time to zoom out.

ZOOM OUT

EXODUS 2:23–25

Find the words "covenant promise" in the verse below and draw a colorful rainbow above them.

23 Years passed, and the king of Egypt died. But the Israelites continued to groan under their burden of slavery. They cried out for help, and their cry rose up to God. 24 God heard their groaning, and he remembered his covenant promise to Abraham, Isaac, and Jacob. 25 He looked down on the people of Israel and knew it was time to act.

Who died?

 _____

Has life gotten any better for God's special people since the villain of our story is no longer alive?

 _____

What are God's people doing?

 _____

What did God remember when He heard their cries for help?

➣ _____

_____

Did you notice the word covenant in this passage? It is an important word, and knowing what it means will help us learn something about Miriam. We don't use it much in modern English, so it is difficult for us to understand it. The simplest definition I can give you is this:

> ·······▶ { covenant: an unbreakable promise of commitment. }

While a covenant is kind of an agreement, it's also a form of unfailing love. The love of God is so strong that even when we make bad mistakes or are sinful, He promises to still love and care for us. A covenant promise is unbreakable. Nothing can stop a covenant-keeping God from taking care of His people. He will always, without fail, help them in their time of need. No matter what! Why?

♥ Because He loves His people all of the time, no matter what!

Now that you know what a covenant promise is, let's think about what meaning it would have for the Israelites who were living in slavery. Write your ideas below.

➣ _____

_____

_____

_____

_____

Any Israelite who loved God and had faith in Him knew about the covenant promise for God to take care of them. That meant they could have faith to believe He would rescue them from slavery! Well, guess what? It was time!

Double underline Exodus 2:25 in today's key Bible passage on page 61.

Now grab all your colors again and turn to your Courage Lessons page at the beginning of your study. Draw a rainbow across the top of the timeline and write "covenant promise" above it. Now every time you look at these pages, you'll remember that God made an unbreakable promise of commitment to care for the Israelites. I hope it also reminds you that you can trust Him.

God knew it was time to make good on His covenant promise. And guess what!?! Miriam was part of His plan to rescue the Israelites.

It's time to zoom in!

ZOOM IN

What does the covenant promise for Israel have to do with Miriam's courage? Well, let's zoom in on Miriam and her family to find out. Moses has been in the desert for 40 years. So it's now been about 80 years since Miriam and her mom had put him into an ark-basket to save his life. She's now old enough to be your great-grandmother!

Remember when we studied Hebrews 11:23–29 during our last Courage Lesson? There was a word that you circled five times. If you remember what it was, write it out below. If you need to, look back at page 49.

_____   _____

_____   _____

_____

Miriam's family had a lot of *that* word! And if you were an Israelite who had a lot of that, you were also very aware of God's covenant promise.

Since Miriam grew up in a house of faith, she believed in the covenant promise of God. That meant she trusted God to take care of her even though things looked really bad. She knew He would come through for her.

Here's the thing: Miriam didn't just have *some* faith. Like the rest of her family, she had a whole lot of it.

Underline Miriam's name and title in the verse below.

Then Miriam the prophetess, the sister of Aaron, took a tambourine in her hand, and all the women went out after her with tambourines and dancing. (Exodus 15:20 ESV)

Miriam was a *prophetess*. That meant that she was a woman who spoke God's Word. She considered what He said to be true. And she knew about His covenant promise. And she taught other people what she learned. Why? Because she believed it!

To be called a prophetess was a *very* special honor! In fact, there are not many women in the Bible who got to use this title.

A PROPHETESS' PUZZLE

} Find the name of these other prophetesses who, like Miriam, are mentioned in the Bible.

DEBORAH (Judges 4:4)   HULDAH (2 Kings 22:14)   ISAIAH'S WIFE (Isaiah 8:3)

ANNA (Luke 2:36)   FOUR DAUGHTERS (Acts 21:9)

```
E Y N F O U R D A U G H T E R S F U
D A W C J M W P B C V A C B W D Q S
E U N C U Y G O I H Y A Z S C X K N
B Q G X B G K N T O T O F H A J Q C
O Z B P B B P Z E R O U Y U L H U U
R F F V N O W Z P R S G B L Y T S C
A R Y G B D L V T D Y X O D R H U C
H P Z F Z R Z T B S I Q Y A P A F Y
I S A I A H S W I F E L L H P N N N
A S O F R L E S C F V L N H J N P L
A B G L N O E V Y N O S Z L M A E J
N L Y K O A Q C R B O J Z C R Z B C
```

For puzzle answers, go to page 110.

How many women, other than Miriam, were called a prophetess? Circle one.

4 ♥ 8 ♥ 309 ♥ 8,000

Because Miriam believed the promises of God and trusted Him to be faithful to them, she was chosen to do something very special. Before I tell you what that was, we have to fast-forward in the story. So let me summarize!

1

God appointed Moses as the leader of Israel and told him to stop hiding in the desert and go back to Egypt, where his brother Aaron would be his helper. He did.

(EXODUS 3:1–4:17)

2

Moses gave Pharaoh a message from God: "Set My people free!" Pharaoh wouldn't do it.

(EXODUS 5:1–2)

3

God sent a whole bunch of bad things to show the evil ruler that the One True God was more powerful than he was. We call those bad things the Ten Plagues. Pharaoh could either let God's special people go or face the consequences.

(EXODUS 7:14–11:10)

PUZZLING PLAGUES }

Find each of the Ten Plagues in the Word Search.

BLOODY RIVER (Exodus 7:14–24)

FROGS (Exodus 7:25–8:15)

LICE (Exodus 8:16–19)

FLIES (Exodus 8:20–32)

LIVESTOCK (Exodus 9:1–7)

SICKNESS (Exodus 9:8–12)

HAIL (Exodus 9:13–25)

LOCUSTS (Exodus 10:1–20)

DARKNESS (Exodus 10:21–29)

DEATH (Exodus 11)

```
X H I D E A T H V R Z B
F L I V E S T O C K V M
U H D H L O C U S T S C
D A R K N E S S T L J R
S I C K N E S S B I T B
H L F L I E S P M C E M
B L O O D Y R I V E R L
O X Y W R E F R O G S P
```

For puzzle answers, go to page 110.

These plagues were terrible. But so was slavery. Using your power to take advantage of another person is always bad, but Pharaoh took things to a whole new level when he started killing baby boys! God sent the plagues to prove His power so that Pharaoh would release the Israelite slaves. Each awful plague was a chance for Pharaoh to see God's power and let the Israelites go free. Each one got scarier and scarier, but Pharaoh still would not let God's people go.

Finally, God had to bring death to every Egyptian house. Sadness covered the land. The grief Pharaoh felt when he found his own lifeless son was enough.

Finally, Pharaoh said to the Israelites, "Get out of here!" (Exodus 12:31–33).

At last, after 400 years of slavery, the ruler of Egypt gave permission for the Israelites to live in freedom. They packed their suitcases. (OK, it was probably baskets that they filled.) They went so fast that they didn't even let the bread rise! They had to leave before Pharaoh changed his mind.

But there was just one little problem. There were a lot of Israelites, and it took organization to get a group of people moving! (Have you ever noticed that when you're on a field trip?)

The verse below tells us how many Israelites left Egypt. Underline the number.

 That night the people of Israel left Rameses and started for Succoth. There were about 600,000 men, plus all the women and children. (Exodus 12:37)

Use a dark pencil that looks like the night sky and circle *when* the people of Israel started their journey.

MICAH 6:4

They were in a big, fat hurry! I mean, they had to pack their entire house and family up, but they left *that night*. And hey, that's a lot of people to organize. Who was in charge of this extra-large field trip? I'm glad you asked!

Circle the names of the three people who God chose to lead the Israelites out of Egypt.

 For I brought you out of Egypt and redeemed you from slavery. I sent Moses, Aaron, and Miriam to help you. (Micah 6:4)

Miriam, the prophetess, was chosen by God to be one of the three people to lead the Israelites to freedom! Now, we've talked a lot about how Moses, the main leader, was Miriam's brother. But do you remember who else was her brother? That's right! Aaron! Imagine! The three leaders were all related. Moses was the leader, Aaron was God's high priest, and Miriam was a prophetess. Do you think it is an accident that all three of them were from a family of exceptional faith? I sure don't!

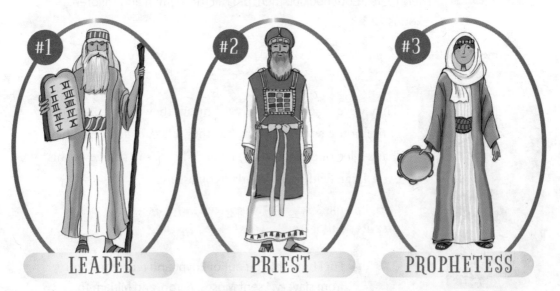

#1 LEADER   #2 PRIEST   #3 PROPHETESS

Turn back to the page at the beginning of the study with your notes on Miriam and label the picture of Moses with "Leader." Then, label Aaron as "Priest." You should have already labeled Miriam as "Prophetess."

We haven't learned much about Aaron yet, but based on what you have been learning about Miriam and Moses, do you think he was ever afraid?

_____

There were probably times that Moses, Aaron, and Miriam were scared out of their minds! Maybe it was when Miriam was sitting by the Nile River, hoping baby Moses did not wake up. Or perhaps it was when Moses was running to the desert away from Egypt, hoping soldiers would not chase after him. Aaron may have felt it when his long-lost brother showed up and said something like, "Hey, do you wanna help everyone bust out and be free?" One way or another, we know that at some point in their lives, all three of these leaders experienced fear.

But to lead well, they couldn't let fear determine how they responded to life. Instead, they had to trust God and do what He told them to do. They had to obey even when it was hard! (Sound familiar?) And that required faith in God. A lot of it.

When God calls us to do something, we cannot rely on how we feel about doing it. No matter how afraid we are, we must trust God and simply do the right thing. Here's COURAGE LESSON #3: A courageous girl chooses to trust God.

Fill in the blank!
Courage Lesson #3:

A courageous girl _____ to _____ _____.

Go back to your **Courage Lessons** page at the beginning of this study.
Beside #3, rewrite the sentence above.

And here's something super cool: When we trust God and have the courage to obey Him, *He sometimes trusts us* to lead. I wonder what exciting things God is preparing you to do as you grow in your courageous obedience!

ZERO IN: What does it mean?

We all feel afraid sometimes, but fear can tell big, fat lies! And those lies can keep you from doing what God wants you to do in your life.

Take for example, Jesus' mother, Mary. When an angel of the Lord came to tell her she was going to be Jesus' mom, she was so afraid. The angel told her not to be afraid and that he was bringing good news. Not bad news. Her fear was putting lies into her heart.

You cannot always trust your emotions. Especially fear.

So what should you do if you feel afraid?

Underline the two things the Bible instructs us to do when we are fearful.

 Say to those with fearful hearts, "Be strong, and do not fear, for your God is coming to destroy your enemies. He is coming to save you." (Isaiah 35:4)

Double underline what God does when we feel fearful.

No matter how important or big your fear may seem, it's important that you don't listen to it. Instead, say something (maybe out loud) to your own fearful heart to remind yourself that God will help you! Sometimes you might feel afraid over something little like jumping off a high dive, but He is with you to even face those kinds of things. God will give you courage! The small stuff is good practice for when He wants you to obey and do *really* scary things. If you keep obeying Him, you'll find that He asks you to do bigger and more important stuff. In short, being courageous enables God to trust *you* as a leader, just like He did with Miriam. How cool is that?

IN MY OWN LIFE

What is one thing that you feel fearful about? Write about it below.

_____

_____

_____

Do you believe that God will take care of you? Why or why not?

_____

_____

_____

_____

_____

According to what you've learned today, what does God want you to do in response to your fear? (Go back and look at Isaiah 35:4.)

_____

_____

_____

_____

_____

How does God want you to obey Him in this situation?

_____

_____

_____

_____

_____

ZIP IT UP: What does God want me to do with it?

The most important thing to do when you feel afraid is to pray.

In today's journal entry, take time to write a prayer to the Lord about any fear you are facing. Ask Him to increase your faith as you obey Him.

Turn to the page at the beginning of this study with your notes on Miriam and her family. Write "faithful" under each of their names because they were full of faith in God, and that was a big part of their courage.

CHAPTER 5

✳ A Courageous Girl Glorifies God

Have you ever had a serious case of stage fright? Imagine you are about to sing a solo in front of a full house! And you're terrified.

You're supposed to sing next, and you have no idea how you'll be able to do it in front of all those people! (You've even tried looking above the audience instead of at them, just like your drama teacher taught you. But you're still sooooo scared!) You can't help asking yourself: *What if I forget the words? What if I sing off-key?*

And then, you decide to pray. "Lord, I'm so nervous! Please help me to trust You. You are the one who gave me my voice and the ability to sing. Help me to use it for Your glory!"

Suddenly, peace washes over you.

You walk out on stage and sing your heart out for Jesus!

I don't know if singing would make you scared, but it sure would terrify me! Experiences like that are just one reason we're learning so much about being brave as we study the life of Miriam.

Go back to the page at the beginning of this study where you're keeping a record of your Courage Lessons and write them below.

⭐ **COURAGE LESSON #1** _____

_____

⭐ **COURAGE LESSON #2** _____

_____

_____

⭐ **COURAGE LESSON #3** _____

_____

Great! Now let's keep digging into God's Word to discover Courage Lesson #4. **Time to start zooming!**

> Zoom In & Out—Who? What? Where? When? Why?

As we mentioned in the last chapter, Miriam is all grown up. In fact, she is old . . . like *really* old! Some people believe she was 90 when Pharaoh finally told the Israelites they were free. This old woman and her two brothers, Moses and Aaron, were chosen by God to lead the Exodus. (That's what we call the Israelites' departure from Egypt. And, of course, the book of the Bible where we've been reading about it is also named after their journey.)

In the last lesson, we learned how the Israelites packed up and left Egypt. Circle the one that best describes it.

They wanted to be careful not to forget anything and have time to say "goodbye" to their Egyptian friends, so they took a month to pack.

Each mom had to run to Wal-Mart for a few supplies and the dads had to finish up some stuff at work, so they left a week after Pharaoh's big announcement.

They packed everything they could fit into their wagons and left that night because they didn't want Pharaoh to change his mind.

You can go back to the last chapter or look up Exodus 12:37 to see if you chose the right answer. (And I think I just heard someone say, "Dannah, there was no Wal-Mart back then!" And . . . you are correct.)

One day they were slaves, and the next night, they were free.

Whew! I'm glad Miriam didn't have to be a slave anymore. I mean, shouldn't old ladies get to sit in squishy chairs and do word searches like this one and relax? Let's imagine what her life might have looked like if she lived today and retired.

MIRIAM'S MAKE-BELIEVE LIFE

} Find all the words below that should have described Miriam's old age and retirement.

TANNING   KNITTING   VACATIONS   GARDENING   READING

```
J  C  S  K  N  I  T  T  I  N  G  C  O  X  D  F  O  O
J  U  T  A  N  N  I  N  G  E  C  P  Y  Z  N  Z  D  N
Q  C  A  Y  E  M  I  P  G  A  R  D  E  N  I  N  G  J
X  L  V  U  M  Z  G  M  I  M  S  V  M  O  H  M  Y  O
L  R  E  A  D  I  N  G  W  X  O  Q  A  Z  I  F  J  R
R  A  K  D  L  Z  N  Z  G  A  E  L  C  M  W  R  U  D
C  E  X  D  D  S  G  K  W  Z  H  T  K  T  G  C  W  R
T  M  V  O  U  N  A  R  V  A  C  A  T  I  O  N  S  F
Z  T  B  B  S  Q  X  O  O  M  X  S  L  K  M  P  R  S
I  P  L  X  F  D  Q  E  S  M  E  X  Y  C  R  J  E  G
T  I  K  Y  G  R  S  M  V  Q  C  H  G  X  S  A  Z  L
A  K  F  R  T  R  A  Z  D  B  L  Y  H  C  S  D  D  E
```

For puzzle answers, go to page 111.

Well, I sure wish it had worked out that way for Miriam, but it didn't.

Let's zoom out to learn what happened next.

ZOOM OUT

EXODUS 14:5–31

Read this amazing story of how God continued to rescue Israel from Pharaoh. Grab a gold or bright yellow pencil. Look for the word "glory" and use your pencil to put sun rays around it every time you see it.

5 When word reached the king of Egypt that the Israelites had fled, Pharaoh and his officials changed their minds. "What have we done, letting all those Israelite slaves get away?" they asked. **6** So Pharaoh harnessed his chariot and called up his troops. **7** He took with him 600 of Egypt's best chariots, along with the rest of the chariots of Egypt, each with its commander. **8** The LORD hardened the heart of Pharaoh, the king of Egypt, so he chased after the people of Israel, who had left with fists raised in defiance. **9** The Egyptians chased after them with all the forces in Pharaoh's army—all his horses and chariots, his charioteers, and his troops. The Egyptians caught up with the people of Israel as they were camped beside the shore near Pi-hahiroth, across from Baal-zephon. **10** As Pharaoh approached, the people of Israel looked up and panicked when they saw the Egyptians overtaking them. They cried out to the LORD, **11** and they said to Moses, "Why did you bring us out here to die in the wilderness? Weren't there enough graves for us in Egypt? What have you done to us? Why did you make us leave Egypt? **12** Didn't we tell you this would happen while we were still in Egypt? We said, 'Leave us alone! Let us be slaves to the Egyptians. It's better to be a slave in Egypt than a corpse in the wilderness!'" **13** But Moses told the people, "Don't be afraid. Just stand still and watch the LORD rescue you today. The Egyptians you see today will never be seen again. **14** The LORD himself will fight for you. Just stay calm." **15** Then the LORD said to Moses, "Why are you crying out to me? Tell the people to get moving! **16** Pick up your staff and raise your hand over the sea. Divide the water so the Israelites can walk through the middle of the sea on dry ground. **17** And I will harden the hearts of the Egyptians, and they will charge in after the Israelites. My great glory will be displayed through Pharaoh and his troops, his chariots, and his charioteers. 18 When my glory

is displayed through them, all Egypt will see my glory and know that I am the LORD!" 19 Then the

angel of God, who had been leading the people of Israel, moved to the rear of the camp. The pillar

of cloud also moved from the front and stood behind them. 20 The cloud settled between the

Egyptian and Israelite camps. As darkness fell, the cloud turned to fire, lighting up the night.

But the Egyptians and Israelites did not approach each other all night. 21 Then Moses raised his

hand over the sea, and the LORD opened up a path through the water with a strong east wind.

The wind blew all that night, turning the seabed into dry land. 22 So the people of Israel walked

through the middle of the sea on dry ground, with walls of water on each side! 23 Then the

Egyptians—all of Pharaoh's horses, chariots, and charioteers—chased them into the middle of the

sea. 24 But just before dawn the LORD looked down on the Egyptian army from the pillar of fire and

cloud, and he threw their forces into total confusion. 25 He twisted their chariot wheels, making

their chariots difficult to drive. "Let's get out of here—away from these Israelites!" the Egyptians

shouted. "The LORD is fighting for them against Egypt!" 26 When all the Israelites had reached the

other side, the LORD said to Moses, "Raise your hand over the sea again. Then the waters will rush

back and cover the Egyptians and their chariots and charioteers." 27 So as the sun began to rise,

Moses raised his hand over the sea, and the water rushed back into its usual place. The Egyptians

tried to escape, but the LORD swept them into the sea. 28 Then the waters returned and covered

all the chariots and charioteers—the entire army of Pharaoh. Of all the Egyptians who had chased

the Israelites into the sea, not a single one survived. 29 But the people of Israel had walked

through the middle of the sea on dry ground, as the water stood up like a wall on both sides.

30 That is how the LORD rescued Israel from the hand of the Egyptians that day. And the Israelites

saw the bodies of the Egyptians washed up on the seashore. 31 When the people of Israel saw

the mighty power that the LORD had unleashed against the Egyptians, they were filled with awe

before him. They put their faith in the LORD and in his servant Moses.

A NOT-SO-FUNNY COMIC STRIP } Draw the four main events described in the passage you just read.

PHARAOH CHANGES HIS MIND & THE EGYPTIANS CHASE THE ISRAELITES

THE ISRAELITES ARE AFRAID & COMPLAIN TO MOSES

3

THE ISRAELITES WALK THROUGH THE RED SEA

4

PHARAOH & HIS CHARIOTS ARE WASHED AWAY IN THE RED SEA

Look back at verses 17 and 18. What does God say the Egyptians saw that day?

⟫―――⟶ _____

_____

_____

What did seeing that help them know?

⟫―――⟶ _____

_____

_____

Read verse 31. Who else saw God's glory that day? And what did they do as a result?

⟫―――⟶ _____

_____

_____

The glory of God is a beautiful thing, but sometimes it can be hard to explain. Don't worry! It's kind of supposed to be that way. Let's just think about it as God's **awesomeness**. His glory was seen by the Egyptians through God's obvious presence with the Israelites. It was displayed in the miracles and plagues that showcased His incredible power! The Egyptians also saw God's glory when He opened the Red Sea for His special people and closed it on their Pharaoh's army. The Israelites saw God's glory, too. As they watched God's power shown to the Egyptians, they began to put their faith in God.

Does it surprise you that they didn't have their faith in God before this? It's sad but true that not every family of Israel was as full of faith as Miriam's was. The plagues of Egypt and this miracle at the Red Sea reminded them of God's power and glory.

ZOOM IN

EXODUS 15:20-21

So now what?! Let's zoom in to see what Miriam's up to on the other side of the Red Sea. **Use your gold or yellow pencil to put a sun ray around the word that looks related to glory.**

20 Then Miriam the prophet, Aaron's sister, took a tambourine and led all the women as they played their tambourines and danced.

21 And Miriam sang this song: "Sing to the LORD, for he has triumphed gloriously; he has hurled both horse and rider into the sea."

Who was Miriam giving credit to for their freedom? Circle one.

Moses (for lifting his hands so high) ♥ **Team Moses-Aaron-Miriam** ♥ **GOD**

How did she give credit?

What was she using? And was she the only one who had this item? If not, who else had theirs?

OK, let me remind you: the Israelites left in a real hurry! They didn't even let their bread rise, remember? They packed the way you might if your house was about to be hit by a hurricane. When you leave *that* quickly, you only pack what you absolutely need to take with you: your food

(because a girl's gotta eat), some basic medicine (in case someone gets wounded), and your undies (at least one extra pair so you can wash them). But you don't pack that super-cute daisy pom-pom that you like to attach to your backpack during the school year because it's soft and cute. You get what I'm saying? Only essentials go with you!!!!

SOOOOOO....
Why did ALLLL these women, including Miriam, pack their tambourines?

⫸───▶ _____

_____

_____

These women packed their instruments of worship on a very, very, very dark night. And if you remember, it was a night of death and sadness. The final plague resulted in the death of the oldest child in each Egyptian home. Even though the Israelites did not experience that in their homes and they were set free, I imagine they knew some of the people who died. And although they wanted to leave Egypt, I would also guess that they were a little afraid of setting off in the night. But these women believed they would need their tambourine to worship God because they trusted Him to bring a bright day WHILE they were surviving a dark night!

Listen to me: A girl who trusts God knows that she'll be singing again even on those dark nights when she doesn't feel like hearing one lonely note of music.

When Miriam left Egypt at night, she didn't know she'd be crossing the Red Sea on dry ground or that Pharaoh's army would be swallowed by the water. But she DID know she'd be worshiping God with that tambourine. That's a lot of faith.

But here's what I really want you to see: Miriam might have been dancing and singing, but it's God who's in the spotlight. She was glorifying Him.

··········▶ { **glorify: to make known or visible.** }

When Miriam sang and danced by the Red Sea, she was telling everyone who deserved all of the credit: God. It was not her courage or Moses's raised hands or Aaron's leadership that was worthy of being glorified. It was God's faithfulness and strength. And that brings us to **COURAGE LESSON # 4: A courageous girl glorifies God!**

Fill in the blank!
Courage Lesson #4:

A courageous girl _____ God!

Go to the **Courage Lessons** page at the beginning of your study.
Beside #4, rewrite the sentence above.

MIRIAM'S REAL LIFE } Now that we know more about Miriam's life, find all the words that *actually* describe Miriam's old age and retirement.

DANCING   COURAGE   SINGING   MIRACLES   WALKING

```
G  K  Y  A  O  H  W  W  S  I  N  G  I  N  G  T  I  Z
X  T  T  V  V  J  H  U  K  T  O  O  V  V  S  M  J  C
S  E  E  B  J  L  B  B  B  X  C  F  S  F  W  I  K  O
T  F  R  O  I  R  L  U  U  X  C  C  W  J  I  R  E  U
C  H  U  X  Y  D  B  D  W  Z  O  U  N  R  X  A  U  R
S  L  S  P  U  W  Y  A  W  A  H  R  K  D  C  C  G  A
A  X  K  Q  A  U  I  N  X  H  L  C  Y  F  M  L  W  G
N  M  Q  A  J  A  N  C  R  W  P  K  E  I  N  E  G  E
C  T  E  Q  D  F  T  I  V  C  W  D  I  P  W  S  D  I
A  I  S  O  M  W  V  N  D  R  V  G  Q  N  E  K  F  I
K  O  Q  B  Y  W  J  G  U  H  X  T  C  F  G  V  D  R
L  B  J  P  V  X  F  T  V  G  R  Y  A  S  N  E  C  M
```

For puzzle answers, go to page 111.

ZERO IN: What does it mean?

A courageous girl celebrates her courage by giving all of the glory to God! She realizes that her courage and strength aren't really her own, but are gifts from God. For that reason, she is thankful and glorifies Him after every courageous act. She gives God credit and that helps other people to know He is present. Sometimes the way she gives God credit is to **WORSHIP!**

But there are lots of ways we can glorify God besides worshiping with a tambourine. I remember a time when I needed a lot of courage. My twin grandbabies, Addie and Zoe, were born so early that they needed to be on special life support in the hospital. They needed oxygen because their lungs were not working without help. Those were some really dark nights!

Every time we stopped praying because we were too tired or started to think things were OK, the oxygen machines told us Addie and Zoe were in danger! So, we prayed harder and asked all of our friends to join us. Every single time we prayed, those sweet babies had good success breathing. Every time.

So we told people: *God did this!* (Because He did!) When we said those three simple words—God did this—we glorified God.

Sometimes it's that simple. (Aren't ya glad you don't need tambourine lessons?)

NanaDannah, Addie & Zoe

Here's a verse that helps me when I feel afraid and need to be reminded that courage comes from trusting God's strength and not my own.

 Don't be afraid, for I am with you. Don't be discouraged, for I am your God. I will strengthen you and help you. I will hold you up with my victorious right hand. (Isaiah 41:10)

As you think about that verse, I need you to know that not all of my prayers have been answered how I hoped they would be. I once prayed very hard for a friend who had cancer. He was not healed, and he died. This verse was important then, too. I thought of it often because I needed God's strength to fight my discouragement and sadness as I grieved. God helped me through that "dark night" too!

IN MY OWN LIFE

Has God helped you through a "dark night" recently? It could be any kind of difficult situation. Write about it below.

_____

_____

_____

_____

_____

_____

Did you trust Him when you were in that difficult time? If not, why? If so, how did that look?

_____

_____

_____

_____

_____

_____

How did you "glorify" God when He helped you through that time? Or how **could** you have "glorified" Him?

⫸———————————————————————————————————

_____

_____

_____

ZIP IT UP: What does God want me to do with it?

If you have a tambourine nearby, grab it. You'll need it after you write your journal entry. I want you to write a song that is as simple as Miriam's. If you need to, you can look at it again in Exodus 15:20–21. Write a two- or three-line song about something God has done for you lately. If you want to, you can sing it out loud.

⫸———————————————————————————————————

_____

_____

_____

_____

_____

_____

Now turn to the page at the beginning of the study with your notes about Miriam. You'll notice that Miriam is a girl in the drawing. How about you update that today?

Draw old-aged Miriam dancing by the Red Sea with a tambourine in her hand. If it's easier, you can just draw a tambourine to remember her heart to glorify God.

✳ Even Courageous Girls Need God's Mercy

Have you ever played Capture the Flag? Imagine you are right now. And, you get stuck in an opposing team's jail for the *entire* game? You wait and wait for one of your teammates to come tag you and set you free.

But they never show up.

You spend the entire game as a prisoner of the enemy. That is not very much fun.

If that really happened, it'd be the longest game of Capture the Flag ever!

Today, as we study our last lesson on the life of Miriam and the story of the Exodus, we see that Miriam is not having much fun either. We will learn that this courageous girl who grew into a courageous woman was also a not-so-perfect human. Like all of us, she was sinful. (Remember how we talked about the truth that courageous people make mistakes and need God's mercy? Well, you're about to see that in Miriam's life.)

Before we dive into our studies, let's review the Courage Lessons you've learned so far. If you need to, look back at your Courage Lessons page at the beginning of the study to help you write them below:

★ **COURAGE LESSON #1** _____

_____

★ **COURAGE LESSON #2** _____

_____

_____

★ **COURAGE LESSON #3** _____

_____

_____

★ **COURAGE LESSON #4** _____

_____

OK, let's start zooming!

▶ *Zoom In & Out—Who? What? Where? When? Why?*

OK, super big brain work is required for what I'm about to tell you! Some people don't learn this until they're in high school or college, but you're ready. Here it is: the story of the Israelites' rescue from Egyptian slavery isn't in the Bible just so that we have a good record of history. There's another reason God put it in Scripture for us. It's there to help us learn about our need to be rescued from sin. Just like God's people were enslaved by Pharaoh, every single one of us can be enslaved or controlled by sin. But the good news is that just like God freed the Israelites, He wants you and me to be free too!

Today we will learn about a big, bad sin in Miriam's life. As we do, we'll really be learning about our own battle with sin. But remember: God likes to set His people free.

Let's zoom out for some *context*!

ZOOM OUT

Today, we'll get context by looking at some Bible verses from the New Testament. Use a black pen to circle every time the words *sin* appears in these verses.

For when we died with Christ, we were set free from the power of sin. . . .

Well then, since God's grace has set us free from the law, does that mean we can go on sinning? Of course not! Don't you realize that you become the slave of whatever you choose to obey? You can be a slave to sin, which leads to death, or you can choose to obey God, which leads to righteous living. Thank God! Once you were slaves to sin, but now you wholeheartedly obey this teaching we have given you. Now you are free from your slavery to sin, and you have become slaves to righteous living. (Romans 6:7, 15–18)

Use the same black pen to underline the words slave or slavery every time they are connected to the word sin. **But use a red pen** to underline the words *slave* or *slavery* when they are connected to righteousness.

Write a summary of what you have learned in these verses.

_____

_____

_____

_____

Each of us has to choose if we will be a slave to sin or if we will obey God's rules for living. The verses you just read tell us that being a slave to sin results in bad things. But choosing to live under God's authority brings good things.

How we live always produces consequences. Sometimes they are bad. For example, if you disobeyed your parents because you wanted more screen time, you might lose your screen. If you fight with your sibling, you might both get a time-out. These are bad consequences.

But consequences can also be good. If you are extra helpful to your mom without even being asked, she might surprise you with an fun ice cream date! (Ice cream is always a happy thing!) That's a good consequence.

Whatever is ruling your life will usually show up in the form of consequences. If you are enslaved by or controlled by sin, you'll have bad stuff happening. If you are obeying God because He is ruling your life, many times there are good rewards for that!

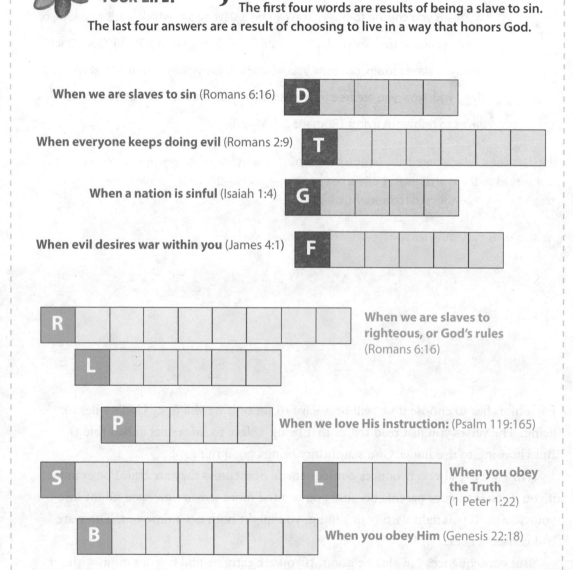

WHAT'S RULING YOUR LIFE? } Fill in the blanks to complete this word puzzle about what happens when we pick what rules our lives.
The first four words are results of being a slave to sin.
The last four answers are a result of choosing to live in a way that honors God.

When we are slaves to sin (Romans 6:16) **D** ☐ ☐ ☐ ☐

When everyone keeps doing evil (Romans 2:9) **T** ☐ ☐ ☐ ☐ ☐ ☐

When a nation is sinful (Isaiah 1:4) **G** ☐ ☐ ☐ ☐

When evil desires war within you (James 4:1) **F** ☐ ☐ ☐ ☐ ☐

R ☐ ☐ ☐ ☐ ☐ ☐ ☐ ☐ When we are slaves to righteous, or God's rules (Romans 6:16)
L ☐ ☐ ☐ ☐ ☐

P ☐ ☐ ☐ ☐ When we love His instruction: (Psalm 119:165)

S ☐ ☐ ☐ ☐ ☐ ☐ **L** ☐ ☐ ☐ When you obey the Truth (1 Peter 1:22)

B ☐ ☐ ☐ ☐ ☐ ☐ When you obey Him (Genesis 22:18)

For puzzle answers, go to page 111.

So, what's ruling your life: sin or God? If you're not sure, think about the consequences you learned about in that puzzle! Which ones are showing up more often?

I hope you find that God rules your life, but sometimes we all struggle with sin being in charge. As we continue learning about Miriam, we'll see that even though she was no longer a slave to Pharaoh, she still had a sin problem. Like us, she needed to choose what ruled her life.

Time to zoom in!

ZOOM IN

Let me set the scene. You've probably heard of the Ten Commandments and might already know the story of God giving them to Moses. You might also know that Aaron and Miriam were in charge of the Israelites while Moses was on the mountain receiving the Ten Commandments from God. One of those commandments was this:

> **The First Commandment:**
> **You must not have any other god but me. (Exodus 20:3)**

Here's where we have a problem. While Moses was talking to God, the Israelites built a golden calf to worship. Why? Well, maybe it was because they had not heard from God in a long time. He was up on that mountain with Moses. But also—and this is important—they were comparing themselves to other people. And everyone else seemed to have idols made out of gold. They wanted one, too! So, after they begged a whole lot, Aaron helped them make one. When Moses came down from the mountain and confronted them, Miriam and Aaron were angry.

This is where we find ourselves in Miriam's story today.

NUMBERS 12:1–16

Grab four highlighters or light-colored pencils or markers. As you read today's verses, pay close attention to what each person says. Highlight the words of Miriam, Aaron, Moses, and God in the colors of your choice. Give each of them their own color so it's easy to see who says what!

1 While they were at Hazeroth, Miriam and Aaron criticized Moses because he had married a Cushite woman. 2 They said, "Has the LORD spoken only through Moses? Hasn't he spoken through us, too?" But the LORD heard them. 3 (Now Moses was very humble—more humble than any other person on earth.) 4 So immediately the LORD called to Moses, Aaron, and Miriam and said, "Go out to the Tabernacle, all three of you!" So the three of them went to the Tabernacle. 5 Then the LORD descended in the pillar of cloud and stood at the entrance of the Tabernacle. "Aaron and Miriam!" he called, and they stepped forward. 6 And the LORD said to them, "Now listen to what I say: "If there were prophets among you, I, the LORD, would reveal myself in visions. I would speak to them in dreams. 7 But not with my servant Moses. Of all my house, he is the one I trust. 8 I speak to him face to face, clearly, and not in riddles! He sees the LORD as he is. So why were you not afraid to criticize my servant Moses?" 9 The LORD was very angry with them, and he departed. 10 As the cloud moved from above the Tabernacle, there stood Miriam, her skin as white as snow from leprosy. When Aaron saw what had happened to her, 11 he cried out to Moses, "Oh, my master! Please don't punish us for this sin we have so foolishly committed. 12 Don't let her be like a stillborn baby, already decayed at birth." 13 So Moses cried out to the LORD, "O God, I beg you, please heal her!" 14 But the LORD said to Moses, "If her father had done nothing more than spit in her face, wouldn't she be defiled for seven days? So keep her outside the camp for seven days, and after that she may be accepted back." 15 So Miriam was kept outside the camp for seven days, and the people waited until she was brought back before they traveled again. 16 Then they left Hazeroth and camped in the wilderness of Paran.

Why did God become angry with Miriam?

What happened to Miriam?

Moses was God's prophet. God chose him and spoke to him. For some reason this was difficult for Miriam and Aaron. (Can you say sibling rivalry?) It's always difficult for us to make room for other people to be first, but when it's a brother or sister . . . well, it can be even more difficult. And, when Miriam and Aaron questioned Moses's authority, God was mad.

When this conflict arose, God gathered Miriam, Aaron, and Moses together (just like your mom or dad might do if epic sibling rivalry broke out in your house). Then, God had to make a decision about who was right. Moses or his brother and sister. God told them clearly that even though Aaron was the high priest and Miriam was a prophetess, Moses was in charge! He was the only one who got to speak to God directly.

What happened next is 100% pure consequence! Miriam got a terrible skin disease called *leprosy*! Why? Because she was living in slavery to her sin. And sin always has consequences.

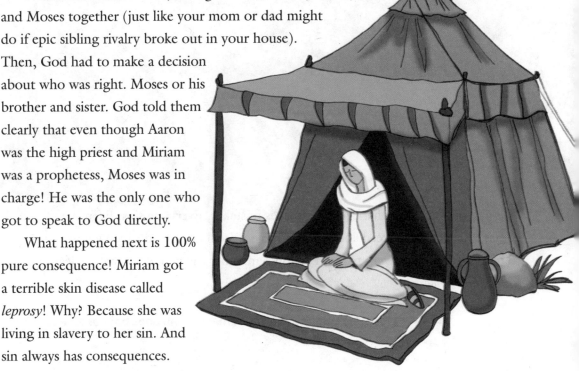

Now, wait a second! Both Miriam *and* Aaron grumbled against Moses. Why didn't Aaron get punished too?

Well, most people think Miriam was the one who started talking bad about Moses first. If you read all of the book of Exodus, you'll learn that Aaron was not a very strong leader. Even though he was the one who usually talked to Pharaoh for Moses, Aaron was typically afraid to speak up. (That's how the people ended up with a golden calf to worship. Aaron would not tell them "no.") Miriam was not afraid to say and do bold things. (That's how her baby brother ended up in the care of his mother instead of an Egyptian princess for the first couple of years or so of his life.)

Sometimes our biggest strengths can quickly become our biggest weaknesses if we aren't careful. And that's exactly what happened with Miriam. Normally, it was a good thing that she had the courage to speak up. But not this time! Now she was sinfully talking without thinking! And God essentially put her in a time-out.

What did Miriam's brothers do when they saw she had leprosy?

➤ _____

_____

_____

What did God do in response to Aaron and Moses?

➤ _____

_____

_____

This just goes to show that everyone makes mistakes. Everyone sins. Even the courageous people we read about in the Bible. We all need God's mercy if we want to be free from our slavery to sin! Do you remember the definition that we learned for the word *mercy*?

········➤ { **mercy: love and compassion for someone who does not deserve it.** }

This leads us to **COURAGE LESSON #5: Courageous people need mercy too!**

Fill in the blank!
Courage Lesson #5:

Courageous people need_____ too!

Go to the **Courage Lessons** page at the beginning of this study.
Beside #5, rewrite the sentence above.

Our heavenly Father is such a good, loving, and wonderful God that He offers us the mercy we need. While there are consequences when we mess up and sin, He doesn't punish us to the full degree or amount that we deserve. And it was because of His mercy that Miriam was healed and allowed back into the Israelite camp. Most people who got leprosy back then never returned because they were too contagious and dangerous to the rest of the people.

But God loved Miriam
♥ all the time, ♥
no matter what.

She was a slave to her sin and had to face the consequences, but God had mercy on her to set her free. Again!

ZERO IN: What does it mean?

The Bible says we all sin (Romans 3:23). So I know you sin. I do too. But, like Miriam, does pride, jealousy, or selfishness ever get the better of you?

Write about a time when you said words you didn't mean, or about a time when you felt jealous or prideful.

_____

_____

_____

_____

_____

_____

How did that situation make you feel?

_____

_____

How does God respond to our sin? Find the words *mercy* and *grace* in the verse below. Circle them.

> But God is so rich in mercy, and he loved us so much, that even though we were dead because of our sins, he gave us life when he raised Christ from the dead. (It is only by God's grace that you have been saved!) (Ephesians 2:4–5)

So how do we receive His mercy? Underline what we need to do in order to receive God's forgiveness.

But if we confess our sins to him, he is faithful and just to forgive us our sins and to cleanse us from all wickedness. (1 John 1:9)

You do not have to be a slave to your sin. Jesus died on the cross to set us free from sin and death. When you sin, confess your sin to God. He will forgive you. That's mercy.

IN MY OWN LIFE

Is there any sin in your life that you haven't confessed to God yet? If so, write it here.

_____

_____

_____

According to the Bible verse we read today (1 John 1:9), what do you need to do in order for God to forgive you?

_____

_____

_____

A courageous girl needs mercy! It's courageous to admit our sin. Why? Because it is the right thing to do. Let's review our big definition for courage:

courage is doing the right thing even when it's hard or you are afraid.

OK, so let's apply this to when *we* sin. What's the right thing to do? Confess it to God. If you want to be freed and forgiven of your sins, that's where you should always begin. Only He has the power to forgive you, and He will.

It's also very helpful to confess it to an adult in your life. Let's look at another verse.

Confess your sins to each other and pray for each other so that you may be healed. The earnest prayer of a righteous person has great power and produces wonderful results. (James 5:16)

Who else should you confess your sin to? Underline the answer in the verse above.

Sometimes it is hard to confess our sin to a person because we find it embarrassing to admit we are wrong. We don't want them to think badly of us. At other times, it just doesn't feel good. In fact, it can feel very, very bad to tell someone else about a sin that you have never admitted. The feeling you have when you want to hide your sin is called *shame*. It's one of the hardest of all our bad emotions to overcome. But just like you don't have to be a slave to sin, you also don't have to be a slave to shame. God's mercy washes it away when you confess your sin.

How does the verse you just read describe the results of confessing your sin to a righteous person?

_____

_____

_____

When we confess our sins to each other, it helps us stop hurting and feeling bad about it. That's one kind of healing we can experience. And the way you feel after you tell someone about sin and they pray with you is, in one word, wonderful.

ZIP IT UP: What does God want me to do with it?

OK, you're almost done with this whole entire study! Wow! We sure have learned a lot of great stuff, haven't we? Let's review it with this fun puzzle!

MIRIAM'S COURAGEOUS ACTS

Use the clues below to fill in the crossword puzzle.
The four ways Miriam was courageous included:

She courageously _ _ _ _ _ _ _ (3)
her baby brother when his life was in danger.

She _ _ _ _ _ _ _ (2)
courage from her parents.

She helped her brothers courageously
_ _ _ _ (4) the people of
Israel out of slavery.

She gave God credit for
her courage by

_ _ _ _ _ _ _ _ _ _ _ (1)
Him with her tambourine
after the Israelites safely crossed the Red Sea.

For puzzle answers, go to page 111.

That's a lot of courage, huh?

I hope you've learned how to be courageous from Miriam. As we end, there's just one more super challenge I'd like you to consider. It may be the most courageous thing you'll ever do, and I hope it will become a regular habit in your life.

Are you ready?

Here goes.

If you feel a lot of shame about a sin you have committed or if you have confessed something to God and still feel ashamed, I want you to tell someone. Your mom. Your dad. Your big sister. Or your children's pastor. These are people who love you and God has placed them in your life to help you. Don't forget that as you put on your courage! You can decide who, but I want you to write them a note or just talk to them about the sin that makes you feel bad.

It takes a lot of courage to tell someone about a sin in your life. But I hope you will learn to do it early. I started to confess my sin to God when I was very young. But I didn't learn to confess my sins to other people until I was in my twenties. I want you to learn to do it sooner than I did.

So, what do ya say? Is there something that makes you feel bad that you wish you could tell someone? Have you confessed a sin to God, but you keep struggling with it? Maybe today is the day that you'll courageously confess your sin to another person. If it is, I hope it is also the day you'll feel the good healing in your heart that God's Word promises.

Use the lines below to write down who you want to talk to and what you want to tell them about.

_____

_____

_____

_____

_____

_____

_____

_____

Now, dear girl, go be courageous! Tell someone and ask them to help you. You will be amazed at how wonderful it feels to be brave about confessing your sin.

I pray that your whole life long, you are a girl of courage. I hope that every time you hear the story of Miriam and the Israelites being set free from Pharaoh, you also remember that Jesus has died to set us free from sin. His mercy is available to us anytime we courageously ask for it.

How Do You Become A Christian?[3]

I'm glad you asked. God loves us so much He sent His Son Jesus to die on the cross for us. Though you might actually know this Bible verse by memory, I want you to read it one more time. It's an important one!

> For this is how God loved the world: He gave his one and only Son, so that everyone who believes in him will not perish but have eternal life. (John 3:16)

Why did Jesus die for us? He died because of our sin.

When we disobey God or choose to do wrong, we sin. Things like being mean, lying, or cheating are examples of sin. The Bible says that every single human who ever walked the earth has sinned. That includes you and me.

Sin separates us from God. And the Bible says the punishment for sin is death. **BUT GOD LOVES US**, so He sent His Son Jesus to die on a cross. The great news is that Jesus didn't stay dead. He came back to life with the power to forgive our sins. And, He offers us the free gift of His salvation.

I don't know about you, but I've never gotten a free gift without having to reach out to accept it. You accept God's free gift of salvation by *believing* in Jesus and *receiving* Him as your Savior.

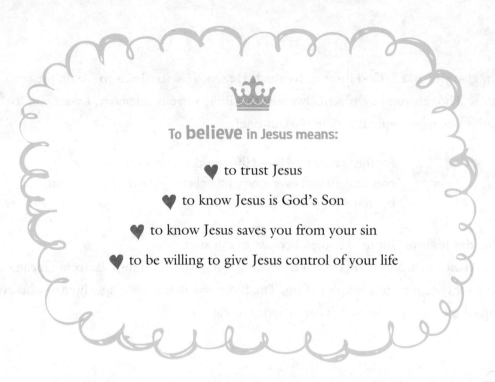

To **believe** in Jesus means:

♥ to trust Jesus

♥ to know Jesus is God's Son

♥ to know Jesus saves you from your sin

♥ to be willing to give Jesus control of your life

Do you believe in Jesus?

If so, you are ready to *receive* Jesus as your Savior, which means you ask Jesus to live inside of you and be in charge of your life. Romans 10:9 reads, "If you openly declare that Jesus is Lord and believe in your heart that God raised him from the dead, you will be saved."

Have you ever received Jesus by asking Him to forgive you of your sins?

If not, would you pray this prayer now?

Dear Lord, I admit to You that I am a sinner.

I thank You for sending Jesus to die on the cross for my sins.

I ask You to forgive me of my sins. I invite You to come into my life

to be my Lord. Thank You for saving me.

In Jesus' name, Amen.

Did you just pray that prayer for the first time?

If so, write the date below.

 The date I became a Christian:

_____

Congratulations!

Now, be sure to tell someone like your mom or your pastor.

They're going to be so excited!

WELCOME TO TRUE GIRL BIBLE STUDY

Mom or Small Group Leader's Guide
For a Six- or Seven-Week Experience

I've not been this excited about teaching tween girls the Bible in a long time! Because Miriam is very close to the age of the girls who will study the Bible using this tool, they will be able to identify with her in a unique way. And one character quality we desperately need in this post-Christian culture is courage.

None of us is born courageous. We learn it from the examples of godly people who imitate God's character. Miriam is a great role model.

And I bet you are, too!

Here's how you can lead your daughter or a small group through this study. You could do it every day in a camp-style setting, but a much more digestible schedule is to tackle one chapter a week. If you're doing your first True Girl Bible study, you might want to schedule seven weeks so you can cover the introduction in the first week. If you're a True Girl Bible study veteran, you could opt to skip the introduction and just schedule six weeks.

God will guide you in the best way to approach your sharing times, but here's what I'd do:

1. Get your own copy of this book and do the homework at the same pace as your daughter or small group. You cannot phone this one in. When I teach one of my own Bible studies online, I also do the homework in real-time so my heart is in tune to what God wants me to learn. In doing so, I'm emotionally and spiritually prepared to guide others through the same content. There's nothing worse than having a Bible study leader who hasn't truly engaged with God's Word in the same intimate way that you have.

2. Select two key conversation questions from each chapter. One can be from a core passage of Scripture in the Zoom In & Out section. This will help you see what they've grappled with mentally in their studies. The second can be from the Zero In section. This will help them share where they need practical and emotional help. Just have fun gabbing about God's Word over your favorite snack or dessert.

3. Pray with your daughter or small group. Based on what they share each week, spend some time praying together. You'll also see greater fruit if you pray for them throughout the week.

Encouraging Bible study for older users. For girls ages 10–12, this book is a challenge but very age appropriate. For far too long, we have been expecting too little of children when they study their Bibles. While I hope this is a fun experience with some puzzles and interactivity, my goal is for them to get a taste for how good it feels to work hard to understand and apply God's Word. Over and over, I'm asked how to make something easier for a tween or a teen. So, before you ask . . . why not try letting them jump in the deep end and experience the thrill!? If they need a life-preserver, send them one, but you might be surprised how well they can swim in the depths of God's Word.

Simplifying the study for younger users. For girls ages 7–9, look for the flower icon. Each time she reaches this, it's time to stop. These icons divide chapters 1–6 into two parts, making one day's worth of homework time shorter and easier to digest. This means that younger girls can schedule two homework sessions each week instead of one so that they finish the chapter at the same time as an older girl.

OK, I feel like I should say this: If you're feeling fearful or believing any lies about your ability to disciple your daughter or a group of girls in this way, strap on your courage! You've got this!

Dannah Gresh
Founder, True Girl

Answers to Puzzles

Answer to "The Good and the Bad Israelites" on page 28:

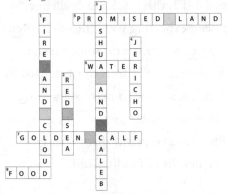

Answer to "Lies vs. Truths about Courage" on page 31:

LIES

1. Courage is doing something extraordinary.
2. Courage is something some people are born with.
3. Courage is something you feel.
4. Courage comes from inside you.
5. Courageous people never make mistakes.

TRUTHS

1. Courage is a character quality you learn from Jesus and others who love Him.
2. Courageous people need God's mercy, too.
3. Courage is a choice to trust God.
4. Courage is living in faithful obedience.
5. Courage comes from God.

Answer to "Courage by the Nile" on page 42:

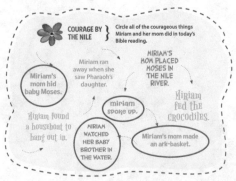

Answer to "The Courage of Moses" on page 51:

Answer to "A Prophetess' Puzzle" on page 64:

```
E Y N F O U R D A U G H T E R S F U
D A W C J M W P B C V A C B W D Q S
E U N C U Y G O I H Y A Z S C X K N
B Q G X B G K N T O T F H A J Q C
O Z B P B B P Z E R O U Y U L H U U
R F F V N O W Z P R S G B L Y T S C
A R Y G B D L V T D Y X O D R H U C
H P Z F Z R Z T B S I Q Y A P A F Y
I S A I A H S W I F E L L H P N N N
A S O F R L E S C F V L N H J N P L
A B G L N O E V Y N O S Z L M A E J
N L Y K O A Q C R B O J Z C R Z B C
```

Answer to "Puzzling Plagues" on page 66:

Answer to *"Miriam's Make-Believe Life"* on page 77:

```
J  C  S  K  N  I  T  T  I  N  G  C  O  X  D  F  O  O
J  U  T  A  N  N  I  N  G  E  C  P  Y  Z  N  Z  D  N
Q  C  A  Y  E  M  I  P  G  A  R  D  E  N  I  N  G  J
X  L  V  U  M  Z  G  M  I  M  S  V  M  O  H  M  Y  O
L  R  E  A  D  I  N  G  W  X  O  Q  A  Z  I  F  J  R
R  A  K  D  L  Z  N  Z  G  A  E  L  C  M  W  R  U  D
C  E  X  D  D  S  G  K  W  Z  H  T  K  T  G  C  W  R
T  M  V  O  U  N  A  R  V  A  C  A  T  I  O  N  S  F
Z  T  B  B  S  Q  X  O  O  M  X  S  L  K  M  P  R  S
I  P  L  X  F  D  Q  E  S  M  E  X  Y  C  R  J  E  G
T  I  K  Y  G  R  S  M  V  Q  C  H  G  X  S  A  Z  L
A  K  F  R  T  R  A  Z  D  B  L  Y  H  C  S  D  D  E
```

Answer to *"Miriam's Courageous Acts"* on page 103:

Answer to *"Miriam's Real Life"* on page 85:

```
G  K  Y  A  O  H  W  W  S  I  N  G  I  N  G  T  I  Z
X  T  T  V  V  J  H  U  K  T  O  O  V  V  S  M  J  C
S  E  E  B  J  L  B  B  B  X  C  F  S  F  W  I  K  O
T  F  R  O  I  R  L  U  U  X  C  C  W  J  I  R  E  U
C  H  U  X  Y  D  B  D  W  Z  O  U  N  R  X  A  U  R
S  L  S  P  U  W  Y  A  W  A  H  R  K  D  C  C  G  A
A  X  K  Q  A  U  I  N  X  H  L  C  Y  F  M  L  W  G
N  M  Q  A  J  A  N  C  R  W  P  K  E  I  N  E  G  E
C  T  E  Q  D  F  T  I  V  C  W  D  I  P  W  S  D  I
A  I  S  O  M  W  V  N  D  R  V  G  Q  N  E  K  F  I
K  O  Q  B  Y  W  J  G  U  H  X  T  C  F  G  V  D  R
L  B  J  P  V  X  F  T  V  G  R  Y  A  S  N  E  C  M
```

Answer to *"What's Ruling Your Life?"* on page 94:

NOTES

1. This introduction is adapted from Dannah Gresh, *Ruth: Becoming a Girl of Loyalty* (Chicago: Moody Publishers, 2001).

2. *Merriam-Webster, s.v.* "extraordinary," https://www.merriam-webster.com/dictionary extraordinary.

3. "How to Be a Christian" section taken from Dannah Gresh, *Lies Girls Believe & The Truth That Sets Them Free* (Chicago: Moody, 2019), 57–59.